D1536949

THINGS TO COME
AND
NOT TO COME

*Bible Prophecy
and Modern Myths*

Aaron Luther Plueger

Published by:

TRUTH versus Truth and Error
12953 California Street
Yucaipa, California 92399-4735

Cover photo credit: National Optical
Astronomy Observatories

First Edition, *Things to Come for Planet Earth*
Plueger, Aaron L. 1926-
Library of Congress Catalog Card Number: 77-23598
International Standard Book Number: 0-570-03762-X

Concordia Publishing House, St. Louis, Missouri
Copyright © 1977 Concordia Publishing House

Manufactured in the United States of America

Second Edition, *Things to Come and Not to Come—Bible Prophecy and Modern Myths*
Plueger, Aaron L. 1926-
Library of Congress Catalog Card Number: 90-70068
International Standard Book Number: 0-9625719-0-3

Publishers: TRUTH versus Truth and Error, Yucaipa, California
Copyright © 1977, 1990 Aaron L. Plueger

Manufactured in the United States of America

First Printing of Second Edition, 1990
Second Printing of Second Edition, 1991
Third Printing of Second Edition, 1995

Contents

Quotations from

Grier, W. J., *Momentous Event*. The Banner of Truth Trust, London, 1945;

Holman Study Bible—Revised Standard Version. A. J. Holman Co., Philadelphia, 1962;

Lowry, Cecil John, *Christian Catechism*. Color Art Press, Oakland, Calif., 1961;

Murray, George L., *Millennial Studies: A Search for Truth*. Baker Book House, Grand Rapids, Mich., 1948;

New American Standard Bible. The Lockman Foundation, La Habra, Calif., and A. J. Holman Co., Philadelphia, 1975;

Pentecost, J. Dwight, *Things to Come*, Dunham Publishing Co., Findlay, Ohio, 1958; reprinted by Zondervan Publishing House, Grand Rapids, Mich.;

Spurgeon, C. H., *The Treasury of the Bible*. Zondervan Publishing House, Grand Rapids, Mich., 1962;

Thomas, L. R., *Does the Bible Teach Millennialism?* Reiner Publications, Swengel, Pa., n. d.;

Young, Edward J., *The Prophecy of Daniel*. Wm. B. Eerdmans Publishing Co., Grand Rapids, Mich., 1949

are used by permission of the publishers.

List of Abbreviations

KJV: King James Version
NKJV: New King James Version
LXX: Septuagint
NASB: New American Standard Bible
NIV: New International Version
RSV: Revised Standard Version
WFB: An American Translation by William F. Beck

List of Charts

Introduction

1988 was the final year for Christ's coming, the world was told. All Christians would be gone, the world was told. Seven years of great tribulation, antichrist, and World War III with Israel defeating Russia were just around the corner, the world was told. King Jesus was about to be enthroned in Jerusalem to reign for a thousand wonderful years, with the saved in risen bodies helping; those who had been left got saved after all; after the millennium, Satan would be released and it would end in rebellion and destruction, the world was told. Was only the date calculation wrong, or is that system of interpretation wrong?

The post-mortem of A.D. 2,000 could have been written in advance. Some, even a few of the early church fathers, had held that the world would last 6,000 years, based on the six "days," of creation, a day to God being as a thousand years. So, the world has been told.

Bible believers by the millions have been and are being painted into a corner by a wrong understanding of prophecy and events of our time. Some religious teachers try to avoid this trap by denying practically all literal Bible teaching.

Francis Pieper and other theologians believe we may be in the time of Satan's release; evidenced also by the present deception of even the elect. To be deceived does not necessarily mean one is lost.

For many, the millennium has come to mean a golden era during which Christ visibly rules the earth—a time of salvation world-wide; of peace, prosperity, long life, happiness, harmony among animals, enormous sizes and amounts of produce; of all knowing God; heaven on earth, almost, for 1,000 years (mille = 1,000; annum = year).

Three differing views of this are postmillennial, premillennial, amillennial. The postmillennial view (a Christ-can't-come-yet error advanced by Daniel Whitby of England, 17th century) is that Christ will return *after* the said golden era of universal gospel triumph—a dream dispelled by our Lord (as in Matthew 13 and 7:13-14).[1] The premillennial, that He returns *before* it. The amillennial, that there is no millennium like that. Amillennialism is quite accurately described by one of its opponents quoting a kindred opponent:

> Its most general character is that of a denial of a literal reign of Christ upon the earth. Satan is conceived as bound at the first coming of

Christ. The present age between the first and second comings is the fulfillment of the millennium. Its adherents differ as to whether the millennium is being fulfilled on the earth (Augustine) or whether it is being fulfilled by the saints in heaven (Warfield). It may be summed up in the idea that there will be no more millennium than there is now, and that the eternal state immediately follows the second coming of Christ. It is similar to postmillennialism in that Christ comes after what they regard as the millennium.[2]

To the premillennial system was added the dispensational view in the 1830's, which divides divine history into eight covenants and seven dispensations, a smoke screen for more serious errors. So, here are four little labels, all in a row: "posties," "premies," "dispies," and "amies." Millennial in the right sense is missing (see page 8).

Several clarifications should be made.

1. "All Dispensationalists are Premillennialists, but not all Premillennialists are Dispensationalists."[3] But nearly all are. Dispensational premillennialism fills the Bible bookstore shelves today.

2. Modern premillennialism should be distinguished from what may be called early premillennialism. It is commonly thought today in premillennial circles that the early church was premillennial. (The reader is referred to chapter 4 for treatment of that question.) Even if such a view was held by some, it needs to be stressed that these early premillennialists, for the most part, had a more spiritualized view of the millennium as a reign of Christ but not necessarily on earth. There were some exceptions, but they were considered extreme. Distinguishing between former errors and more recent ones, Murray writes:

> This premillennialism is not the Chiliasm of the early Church, but something which first appeared early in the nineteenth century. It is a premillennialism wedded to dispensationalism.[4]

He is referring to the "revelations" of the 1830s, which began the succession of Irving-Darby-Blackstone-Scofield-Lindsey (Chapter 11 herein). Early premillennialism was described in much milder terms than today's view which goes by that name. It was more innocent. It was not so speculative; there was no secret rapture; no seven-year tribulation; and no restoration of national Israel. The church, composed of all races, was considered the true Israel. William Cox correctly observes that "there is very little resemblance between historic premillennialism and the premillennialism of our time."[5]

7

3. Dispensationalism is a distraction. Although much attention is focused upon it in this book, its additions to premillennialism are of no ultimate consequence compared to its premillennial core. Premillennialism remains the prime deception, with its two comings of Christ (FOR then WITH the saints), its salvation after Christ comes, and its separate resurrection/judgment days for righteous and for wicked.

A spin in 1994, "*progressive* dispensationalism," still is basic premillennialism. Its associating the promises to Israel "more" closely with the Church; its acknowledging "more continuity" in God's plan; its seeing God's promises to Abraham "more" in relation to all nations, Jesus and the Spirit being an "initial realization" of old Israel's restoration, and its less insistence on a *pre*tribulational rapture, plus other downplayings, makes it a less obvious but no less dangerous threat to the faith once delivered to the saints.

That once-for-all faith (theology), is not progressive. New Testament prophetic fulfillment is progressive only in the sense of deepening and extent.

4. "Amillennial" is a misleading label, as if one denies Revelation 20. It gives errorists opportunity to ensnare the unprepared and turns Bible believers away from amillennial churches. The issue is not whether there is a millennium. The question is rather, *what is* it and *when is* it? Cox states the situation clearly:

> Amillennialism literally means "no millennium." This is an unfortunate term, however, since the great majority of amillennialists definitely do believe in a millennium based on Revelation 20:1-10. They simply rebel against the hyperliteralism placed on this passage by most of the other schools of millennialism. Amillennialists interpret Revelation 20:1-10 as representing the period of time between the two advents of our Lord, that is, as going on at the present time and ending when our Lord returns.[6]

Such church bodies should get shorn of the label "Amillennial" and use Millennial, thus putting the onus on Post-, Pre- and Dispensational. More millennium than now? Who needs it? Cox cites "the wag" who coined "pan-millennial"—all "will pan out" as God wants.[7]

With a subject as vast as the last things it is necessary to set some boundaries. The objective of this book is to give a rather comprehensive treatment of last things and the problem areas of interpretation. Of course one cannot, need not, and should not be exhaustive. One *cannot* be exhaustive, because time and the sheer volume of material involved do not allow it. It would take more worlds than this, to borrow from the imagery of John 21:25, to contain all that might be written. This writer's library section on this subject is quite voluminous. Many sources were not quoted in the interest of selectivity, brevity, and preciseness. One *need not* be exhaustive. After all, four examples demonstrate as effectively as would forty-four. As with effective painting, what is omitted requires as much good judgment as what is included. Every major passage and theme on things to come is treated. Representative arguments are employed instead of dealing with each Scripture bearing on the same point. The reader should make his own applications to related passages. One *should not* be exhaustive, because it would be exhausting both for the writer and for the reader. This is a weakness of much prophetic literature. There is a reason why Hal Lindsey's *The Late Great Planet Earth* has been translated into dozens of languages—it really does not contain much theology but is current, interesting, and to the point, though a mixture of truth and error.

The teaching of Jesus on things to come is presented in chapter 1. The material of chapters 2-4 is arranged according to historical sequence, that is, Old Testament, apostles, church. Chapters 5-14 discuss various related topics.

The index of Scripture references should prove helpful to the reader, but bear in mind that, as in all sound theology, the parts should be interpreted in light of the whole.

Things to Come and Not to Come is a corrective work, not sensational predictions. This book lets the Book show that ever since Christ's ascension there has been just one awesome event ahead for this world, as the creeds of the apostolic, historic church have taught for centuries, namely, Christ's return at the end of the world, which will usher in the eternal realms. Signs of its approach abound. Every day brings it closer.

A thrilling adventure awaits in this thorough yet concise compendium of what Jesus, His apostles, and His church have taught. By rediscovery, the reader will rejoice in renewed expectation and stability, so needed in these days of speculation.

Read on!

CHAPTER 1

Things to Come
According to the Coming One

It seems almost impertinent to speak of the teaching of Jesus as if one were comparing His opinion with that of others. For the Christian the words of Jesus are not just opinion. They are the final word. What He says, being God, is altogether decisive. "For the testimony of Jesus is the spirit of prophecy" (Revelation 19:10). He says, "The Scriptures . . . bear witness of Me" (John 5:39). All Biblical revelation, all history, everything converges in Him and is given direction from Him, even as the cornerstone. He is *the* Word.

Just as the first commandment in essence embodies and comprises all the others, so what Jesus says is the basis of everything. Did not the Father at the Transfiguration testify from heaven saying, "This is My beloved Son, with whom I am well pleased; listen to Him" (Matthew 17:5 RSV). The fact that the Son of God was to be the source of all key revelation is seen also from the words of the woman who came to the well in Samaria to draw water. During her conversation with Jesus she said, "I know that Messiah is coming (He who is called Christ); when He comes He will show us all things" (John 4:25 RSV). He is indeed the light so that no one need be in darkness or misled. Jesus says that the wise build on "these words of Mine" (Matthew 7:24).

Jesus Christ . . . is the very substance, marrow, soul and scope of the whole Scriptures. What are the whole Scriptures, but as it were the spiritual swadling clothes of the Holy child Jesus. (1) Christ is the truth and substance of all types and shadows. (2) Christ is the matter and substance of the Covenant of Grace under all administrations thereof; under the Old Testament Christ is *veyled,* under the New Covenant *revealed.* (3) Christ is the centre and meeting place of all the promises, for in Him all the promises of God are Yea, and they are Amen. (4) Christ is the thing signified, sealed, and exhibited in all the sacraments of the Old and New Testaments, whether ordinary or extraordinary. (5) Scripture genealogies are to lead us on to the true line of Christ. (6) Scripture chronologies are to discover to us the times and seasons of Christ. (7) Scripture laws are our schoolmaster to bring us to Christ; the moral by correcting, the ceremonial by directing. And (8) Scripture gospel is Christ's light, whereby we know him; Christ's voice whereby we hear and follow Him; Christ's cords of love, whereby we are drawn into sweet union and communion with Him; yea, it is the power of God unto salvation unto all them that believe in Christ Jesus. Keep therefore still Jesus Christ in your eye, in the perusal of the Scripture, as the end, scope, and substance thereof. For as the sun gives light to all the heavenly bodies, so Jesus Christ the Sun of righteousness gives light to all the Holy Scriptures.[1]

Does Jesus teach worldly 1,000 year millennialism? The post- pre- and dispie systems say Yes. The latter gets the camel's nose under the tent by a "kingdom" distinction, explained as follows:

A Survey of the Gospels and Acts 1

Matthew—Mark. After his baptism Jesus began His ministry, proclaiming, "Repent; for the kingdom of heaven is at hand" (Matthew 4:17). It is vital to understand (1) what He meant by the kingdom of heaven (lit. "of the heavens," non-worldly), and (2) that it was at hand.

1. Dispensationalists divide the "kingdom of God" from the "kingdom of heaven." They "build much of their argument upon the assumption that the kingdom of God and the kingdom of heaven are two separate kingdoms,"[2] saying that the one is Gentile and current, while the other is Jewish and postponed. But many Bible passages use the terms interchangeably! This is how some concoct a difference:

> In the Gospel according to Matthew this kingdom is designated in the main as the kingdom of heaven, whereas the kingdom of God is mentioned but a few times. . . . Mark and Luke, on the other hand, are writing to Gentiles, so they use the phrase "kingdom of God" rather than the other.[3]

Several Scriptures will suffice to show the inconsistency of this idea. "Jesus came . . . saying, '. . . The kingdom of God is at hand . . . (Mark 1:15).' " The parallel is Matthew 4:17: "The kingdom of heaven is at hand." Note that the terms "kingdom of God" and "kingdom of heaven" are used interchangeably and with the same audience—and this by inspiration of the Holy Spirit. Even more telling is an example of our Lord's usage of both terms in the same breath (see also the parallels, Matthew 19:14 and Mark 10:14):

Jesus said to His disciples, "Truly I say to you, it is hard for a rich man to enter the *kingdom of heaven*. And again I say to you, it is easier for a camel to go through the eye of a needle, than for a rich man to enter the *kingdom of God* (Matthew 19:23-24).

Surely no one would try to divide between this utterance as if in the first half He spoke of a rich Jew, and in the second a rich Gentile. The different terms used by God the Son for the *same* kingdom, ends this two-kingdom falsehood; so seeing, disputants must answer to Him!

Often "kingdom" stands alone, showing all terms to mean the same. Making them two has an "ulterior motive" (page 19). Making "of God" sometimes include "of heaven" is to cover up contradictions.

Before one can correctly understand the teachings of Scripture concerning God's kingdom, the fact must be established that God has but *one* kingdom. While this kingdom is referred to by different terms in the Bible (kingdom of God, kingdom of heaven, kingdom of our Lord, kingdom of Christ), all such terms are used interchangeably, and each term is synonymous, describing one and the same eternal kingdom.[4]

2. The kingdom was and is "at hand" in Him.[5] "He has delivered us from the dominion of darkness and transferred us to the kingdom of his beloved Son (Colossians 1:13)." People are now in it. For the non-materialistic nature of that kingdom, let this suffice: "The kingdom of God is not eating and drinking, but righteousness and peace and joy in the Holy Spirit" (Romans 14:17).[6] The kingdom is not materialistic, but no less real. It is substantial and enduring, to be enjoyed at last in resurrected bodies.

Contrary to the clear words of Jesus and the Scriptures, dispensationalism teaches that Christ came to establish a theocratic, earthly kingdom, that He offered Himself as king to the Jewish people, but that that offer was refused, and so the kingdom was postponed. Such an idea raises serious problems. For one thing, the Jewish people were under Rome at the time. When faced with the "king of the Jews" accusation, the Lord answered Pilate, "My kingdom is not of this world. . . . My kingdom is not of this realm" (John 18:36). Another difficulty in interpreting the kingdom dispensationally is encountered with Christ's own declarations as to His mission, e.g., "The Son of Man did not come to be served, but to serve and to give His life as a ransom for many" (Mark 10:45). "Such statements," it is observed, "cannot be reconciled with the Dispensational scheme."[7] Such a scheme meets further difficulty in the fact that Jesus refused that kingship. "Jesus therefore perceiving that they were intending to come and take Him by force to make Him king, withdrew again to the mountain by Himself alone" (John 6:15). As for His triumphal entry into Jerusalem (Matthew 21; Mark 11; Luke 19; John 12), it was not as in the Scofield Bible heading of Matthew 21: "The King's public offer of himself as King,"[8] but an accepting of worship as the true heavenly king. These and other insuperable difficulties abound—notably a pre-Calvary unredeemed kingdom—if the kingdom progression is thought to have taken this route.

> To the Christian who realizes the meaning of the Cross, who knows that he has been redeemed by the precious blood of Christ, the question raised by the Dispensational interpretation of the words "at hand" is of the greatest moment. It amounts to this, Could men have been saved without the Cross?[9]

And as for a kingdom *postponement,* note what happens to those who refuse Christ as Savior, be they Jew or Gentile, e.g., as described in Luke 19:11–27 in Christ's parable of the nobleman who left to receive a kingdom, returned, and ordered all rebels slain!

Christ's teaching regarding the course of world history allows for no dispensational break of progression from His earthly ministry to His final advent.

> In the parables of the wheat and tares and of the net (Matthew 13:24–30, 36–43, and 47–50), the Lord is giving, as all admit, a picture of this gospel age, which closes with His second coming. In the kingdom, the wheat and the tares are to grow together till the harvest at the end of the world.[10]

Note the parable of the net from the same chapter:

> Again, the kingdom of heaven is like a drag-net cast into the sea, and gathering fish of every kind; and when it was filled, they drew it up on the beach; and they sat down, and gathered the good fish into containers, but the bad they threw away. So it will be at the end of the universe (Gk. aionos); the angels shall come forth, and sever the wicked from among the righteous, and will cast them into the furnace of fire; there shall be weeping and gnashing of teeth (Matthew 13:47-50).

Once again, observe the unbroken progression without dispensations, and that the "kingdom of heaven" continues until heaven.

The Savior speaks from his time then in the first century A.D. and spans all-inclusive history to the *physical* end of the world, with no mention of interruption or a 1,000 year kingdom intervening. In our survey of Matthew-Mark we come now to Matthew 16:24–28 and 19:27–29, passages similar in content:

> Then Jesus said to His disciples, "If anyone wishes to come after Me, let him deny himself, and take up his cross, and follow Me. For whoever wishes to save his life shall lose it; but whoever loses his life for My sake shall find it. For what will a man be profited, if he gains the whole world, and forfeits his soul? Or what will a man give in exchange for his soul? For the Son of Man is going to come in the glory of His father with His angels; and will then recompense every man according to his deeds. Truly I say to you, there are some of those who are standing here who shall not taste death until they see the Son of Man coming in His kingdom."
>
> Then Peter answered and said to Him, "Behold, we have left everything and followed You; what then will there be for us?" And Jesus said to them, "Truly I say to you, that you who have followed Me, in the regeneration when the Son of Man will sit on His glorious throne, you also shall sit upon twelve thrones, judging the twelve tribes of Israel."

Note that the closing verse in the former example would have been proved incorrect if the "kingdom" were an earthly Palestine. It must refer rather to a nonpersonal manifestation, a coming in His kingdom "in power" (Mark 9:1) such as experienced at Pentecost, or in the destruction of Jerusalem. But the point to be observed is the unbroken movement toward the final recompense. The second reference above may seem to lend credence to the idea of some special kingdom— "twelve thrones, judging the twelve tribes"[11]—however, it need not mean that, for it does not suggest an intervening period, but a final judgment, and is just as true if so applied. There are other wondrous matters to ponder concerning the judgment, a many-sided theme. For instance, 1 Corinthians 6:2–3: "Or do you not know that the saints will judge the world? . . . Do you not know that we shall judge angels?"

Another insight into the eschatology of our Lord regarding His own Jewish people is given in the parable of the wicked tenant farmers, Matthew 21:33–44, a parable foretelling His rejection. When he comes, the wicked will not be given the kingdom but will suffer a wretched end. Further, the words "journey" and "harvest time" show that the meaning cannot be confined to the A.D. 70 destruction but suggest even more strongly the final end.

The next chapter's parable of the marriage feast (22:1–14) ends with no mention of a coming kingdom age, but rather with missing out forever for those who refuse or those who come on their own terms.

In Matthew 23:39 Jesus says, ". . . you shall not see Me until you say, 'Blessed is He who comes in the name of the Lord.' " This "until," does not mean thereafter a conversion of Jewry. When He comes the unsaved must acknowledge Him too late. Isaiah 45:23–24 declares, "To Me every knee shall bow, every tongue shall swear . . . to Him shall come and be ashamed all who were incensed against Him"; Philippians 2:10 adds "at the name of Jesus." Now only may any be saved:

> But their minds were hardened; for until this very day at the reading of the old covenant the same veil remains unlifted, because it is removed in Christ. But to this day whenever Moses is read, a veil lies over their heart; but whenever a man turns to the Lord, the veil is taken away (2 Corinthians 3:14–16).

The veil fell away from many Jews in that day as it has for many Jews in this day. Even Jewish historians have estimated there were nearly two million Jewish converts to Christianity during the first century after Christ. When they look on the pierced One (John 19:37), they are gathered "the way a hen gathers her chicks under her wings" (Matthew 23:37). This is exactly the thought brought out by Peter with John at the Beautiful Gate of the temple:

> "Men of Israel, why do you marvel at this, or why do you gaze at us, as if by our own power or piety we had made him walk? . . . God . . . has glorified . . . Jesus, the one whom you delivered up, and disowned in the presence of Pilate. . . . But the things which God announced beforehand by the mouth of all the prophets, that His Christ should suffer, He has thus fulfilled. Repent therefore and return, that your sins may be wiped away, in order that times of refreshing may come from the presence of the Lord; and that He may send Jesus, the Christ appointed for you, whom heaven must receive until the period of restoration of all things about which God spoke by the mouth of His holy prophets from ancient time. Moses said, "The Lord God shall raise up for you a prophet like me from your brethren: to Him you shall give heed in everything He says to you. And it shall be that every soul that does not heed that prophet shall be utterly destroyed from among the people.' And likewise, all the prophets who have spoken,

from Samuel and his successors onward, also announced these days. It is you who are the sons of the prophets, and of the covenant which God made with your fathers, saying to Abraham, 'And in your seed all the families of the earth shall be blessed.' For you first, God raised up His Servant, and sent Him to bless you by turning every one of you from your wicked ways" (Acts 3:12–26).

How merciful and loving that God sent God the Son into the world. This promised Savior for all was raised up (resurrection not meant in Acts 3:26 above) and first "sent . . . to the lost sheep of the house of Israel" (Matthew 15:24). After her miraculous conception by the power of the Holy Spirit, Mary said: "My soul magnifies the Lord and my spirit has rejoiced in God my Savior . . . He has helped His servant Israel, in remembrance of His mercy, as He spoke to our fathers, to Abraham and to his seed forever" (Luke 1:46–47, 54–55 NKJV). How unspeakably gracious of the Savior, even after the Jewish rejection and sharing in His crucifixion, to direct that the apostles preach the gospel to all the world *beginning at Jerusalem.* Just so, in the text above, Peter with John entreated them and with a warning urged them to repent and turn from their wicked ways before His second coming at the times of restitution when it would be too late.

Many today interpret Acts 3:21, "times of restitution," as meaning a restoration of the Jewry of old to "yet . . . her greatest earthly exaltation and glory" (Scofield note to Romans 11:26). Dispensational teaching makes the Jewish people in the future the light of the world instead of the Jewish Savior. The historic faith, however, does not agree with such futurism. It sees Isaiah 60:1–3 and similar prophecies being wonderfully fulfilled starting from the Messiah's mission and the apostolic outreach. The Savior's light has shown out across the centuries from that beginning in Palestine; thus a billion believers now, mostly *Gentiles,* look to those Jewish roots from which the Savior and Word of God arose. "Arise, shine; for thy light is come . . . and the *Gentiles* shall come to thy light, and kings to the brightness of thy rising" (Isaiah 60:1,3 KJV)—Magi, Roman emperor, Europe's kings and queens, presidents, chiefs—fulfilled indeed!

Yet dispensationalism always interprets such passages and Acts 3:21 (above) as referring to "days when Jerusalem has been made the center of earth's worship . . . the Jew will then be the missionary, and to the very 'nations' now called 'Christian'!" (Scofield's note on Zechariah 8:23). In that verse, Jerome discerns "the garment of a Jewish man" to mean the Messiah. People today still yearn to touch the hem of

His garment (Matthew 9:21; Mark 6:56). More than that interpretation is involved of course, for "salvation is of the Jews" (Jesus, John 4:22). It commenced in Jerusalem; its apostles were Jewish; the Savior himself was of the seed of David. In Chapter 14, more will be said on why "the restitution of all things" is not a second special dealing with people of Jewish roots.

At Matthew 24 one stands before a great body of prophetic truth uttered by our Lord. In approaching it, one should bear in mind that a prophecy can have a near and a far fulfillment, as Ramm says: "The destruction of Jerusalem is prophesied by our Lord and through it we have a perspective through which to envision the end of the world."[12] In Matthew 24:3 the disciples inquire as to His coming and the end of the aionos—(Greek) meaning not "age" only but *the universe!* The same word is used also in Hebrews 11:3 for created *substance,* and worlds, 1:2. Beware. End of the age and end of the world mean the same!

Verses 9-14 sketch the general course of the world. Note that there is no break anywhere from that day to the end. Verse 14 needs comment: "And this gospel of the kingdom shall be preached in the whole world for a witness to all the nations, and then the end shall come." The "gospel of the kingdom" is not a different *form* (Scofield) of gospel, as if the bloodless, millennial, unsaving dispie "kingdom of heaven" gospel is not damned by Galatians 1:8-9. Parallels such as Matthew 4:23 and Mark 1:14 show that the "kingdom of heaven" and "kingdom of God" gospel is the same "form." World-wide preaching of the one and only gospel stands fulfilled (see pages 87-88). A future 7 or 1,007 year preaching of "kingdom" gospel is falsehood.

Verse 15: "When you see the abomination of desolation which was spoken of through Daniel the prophet, standing in the holy place...." This verse may be understood as referring to the destruction of Jerusalem in A.D. 70.

The "abomination of desolation" is a Hebrew expression, signifying "abominable, or hateful destroyer." Where Daniel uses the word abomination, Christ adds the word "desolation," because it was to make Jerusalem utterly desolate. As Luke in this connection speaks of the compassing of Jerusalem with armies, I think it clear that, by the abomination of desolation, the Savior meant to designate the Roman armies. These were composed of soldiers who were idolators. They carried in front of their legions ensigns or standards upon which were painted the images of eagles and of their emperors. These, Suetonius informs us, the Romans worshipped . . . In corroboration of the fact that the Romans worshipped these standards, Josephus adds, "that af-

17

ter the city was taken, the Romans brought their ensigns into the temple, and placed them opposite the eastern gate, and sacrificed to them in that place."[13]

A most enlightening explanation along the same lines is given in a lengthy excerpt from Eusebius, bishop of Caesarea, born about A.D. 260:

> The whole body, however, of the church of Jerusalem, having been commanded by a divine revelation, given to men of approved piety there before the war, removed from the city, and dwelt at a certain town beyond the Jordan, called Pella. Here, those that believed in Christ, having removed from Jerusalem, as if holy men had entirely abandoned the royal city itself, and the whole land of Judea . . . when, finally, the abomination of desolation, according to the prophetic declaration, stood in the very temple of God, so celebrated of old, but which now was approaching its total downfall and final destruction by fire; all this, I say, any one that wishes may see accurately stated in the history written by Josephus.[14]

Comments on the Change of Covenants at Calvary. As Christ had done, so did the apostles instruct Jewish hearers that He, God the Son, His coming, and His universal kingdom or church, were Divinely ordained in fulfillment of prophecy, and that the end of literal Israel also was according to prophecy. Matthew Henry's Commentary, still the most widely used, explains that there was no way to abolish the Mosaiac economy but by destroying the temple, and the holy city, and the Levitical priesthood, and that whole nation which so incurably doted on them. The Bible clearly reveals this, as in Hebrews 8:13—"In speaking of a new covenant he treats the first as obsolete. And what is becoming obsolete and growing old is ready to vanish away," or in 10:9—"He abolishes the first in order to establish the second" (RSV).

As in the Old Covenant, so in the New, the people of God are called out for a definite purpose—compare Exodus 19:5-6 with 1 Peter 2:9. The people of Israel, a prototype of the New Testament church, were designated by similar terms; for example, the Greek translation (LXX) of 1 Samuel 17:47 by seventy Jewish scholars uses EKKLESIA, church, for Israel. Rightly understood, the church began in Eden.

Thus the church has a past (carnal), a present (spiritual), and a future (heavenly). Restorationism is out. The kingdom cannot return to Mosaism, nor stop its change to glory. So the church since Eden sings, "We're marching upward to Zion, the beautiful city of God."

18

Satan's postponement myth (pages 11-12) defies Jesus in Matthew 16:18-19: "Church" and "kingdom of heaven" are inseparable! Hebrews 12:22-23 denies postponement; the "CHURCH" is His visible kingdom, superceding old Zion and old Jerusalem forever. The church was founded in eternity as are the chosen. Abraham's seed first contained the Jewish people but was to include believers of all nations as "the Israel of God (Galatians 6:15-16)." The "mystery (Ephesians 3:3,6)" was not that the Gentiles were to be saved, but that Jews and Gentiles were to be one body in Christ! Racist lines are gone forever in Him. Dispensationalism is done away. Who said? Our Lord Jesus Christ: "Other sheep I have, which are not of this (Jewish) fold: them also I must bring . . . there shall be one fold, one shepherd (John 10:16)."

Verse 21 speaks of "great tribulation." This is a reference to the pre-A.D. 70 generation and a prophecy of the end time—the former evident in verse 20: ". . . your flight . . . in the winter, or on a Sabbath," the latter evident in verses 22 ff., the meaning of which cannot be confined to that day but extends to the end of the world.

Compare verses 27-28 with Luke 17:20-37 which intertwines A.D. 70 and the end. The "eagles" suggest Roman army insignia, or as vultures by instinct zero in on a body, so with the saints toward Christ.

Verse 29: *"Immediately* after the tribulation of those days," the universe disintegrates, sun and moon are put out, the stars fall. (No future millennium.) In that same awesome moment—verses 30-31—all nations mourn (Jewish too) as they see the Son of Man coming in power and great glory, dispatching angels with loud trumpet to gather the elect. The Principal of a Bible Institute teaching dispensationalism, saw his error and wrote:

> The Bible, the church Fathers, the Great Historic Church Creeds, the Great Reformers, the true teachers everywhere teach but one future bodily coming, the Second Advent, which is visible and noisy. I Thess. 4:14-17; 2 Peter 3:10-17. This is the Rapture of the Church. Christ will come at that time (on the last day) with His Church, and for His Church; angels and the souls of departed saints will accompany Him as He descends from Heaven; at the sound of the trumpet, as Christ descends, the souls of the righteous dead are reunited with their bodies (this is the resurrection day), the saints living upon earth shall suddenly be changed and, together with the resurrected, shall arise to meet Him in the air to accompany Him to earth when He executes judgment upon the wicked. They shall forever be with Him. Hebrews 9:28; John 5:28, 29; 1 Cor. 6:2; 15:51-56; 1 Thess. 3:13; 4:14-17; Jude 14; Rev. 1:7.[15]

Again it should be noted that in all the prophetic teaching of this chapter Christ never speaks of an intervening earthly kingdom age. Furthermore, He tells of the days of Noah and of Lot, with one taken and another left (in the destruction). The parallel in Luke 17:20-37 intertwines A.D. 70 and the end. This points up the fact that there is nothing such as a rapture and earthly millennium coming between that time (when these words were spoken) and the end.

Verse 34: "Verily I say unto you, This generation shall not pass till all these things be fulfilled" (KJV). See page 74. He says to the Twelve, "When *you* see (verse 33)" - their A.D. 33 generation was included.

Verse 36: "Of that day and hour knows no one, no, not the angels of heaven, but my Father only." Mark 13:32, "neither the Son, but the Father." The Father alone knows the when, says Jesus the Son; neither the Bible, nor the Holy Spirit, nor developing events, can reveal the final century. Prophecy, like a suit, fits all generations—the last one perfectly, but unknown. St. Augustine said: "That day lies hid, that every day we may be on the watch." On verses 40-42, see page 67.

The three parables of Matthew 25 (Ten Virgins, Talents, Judgment) stress preparedness and reward or loss, issuing in final destinies of either everlasting punishment or everlasting life. Unless something is imported from the outside and made to complicate the simplicity of these teachings, one would understand only an unbroken progression to a single final coming; nor would one find in these parables a complicated, confusing distinction between Jews and Gentiles.

In Matthew 26:29 Jesus speaks of his not again drinking "of this fruit of the vine until that day when I drink it new with you in My Father's kingdom." The parallels in Mark and Luke quote the Lord as saying "kingdom of God." See former proofs in this chapter showing that terms such as kingdom, kingdom of heaven, kingdom of God, kingdom of Christ, kingdom of our Lord, the Father's kingdom, "the kingdom of Christ and of God" (Ephesians 5:5), mean the same kingdom.

Finally, the Great Commission of Matthew 28 extends to the close of the age, without mention of any other age coming before eternity. It contains also our Lord's tremendous declaration, "All authority *has been* given to Me in heaven *and on earth*" (verse 18)—AT PRESENT is his pre-eternity reign. Lawrence Thomas well remarks:

> After His resurrection Jesus said, "All power (authority, R.S.V.) is given unto Me in heaven and in earth" (Matthew 28:18). How much power and authority? "All!" Where? "In heaven and in earth!"[16]

Luke. As a synoptic gospel, Luke requires little additional treatment in this survey. References to various parallel passages have been made already.

It may be noted in the annunciation to Mary that "the throne of David" is mentioned, and "the house of Jacob" and that "of His kingdom there will be no end." This cannot refer to a kingdom age of limited duration. "His Kingdom is never said to be a 1,000-year Kingdom, but always an everlasting Kingdom."[17]

Reference has been made previously to Luke 17 and how clearly the Savior sets forth therein that the day of grace continues from His first advent to the day of destruction, uninterrupted by a 1,000-year rule over the earth administered by Him from a Palestinian headquarters at Jerusalem.

Also, in this chapter we have treated Luke 21 in connection with its Matthew 24 and Mark 13 parallels. Luke 21:24 needs further comment:

> They will fall by the edge of the sword, and will be led captive into all the nations; and Jerusalem will be trampled underfoot by the Gentiles until the times of the Gentiles be fulfilled.

Once again it must be said that neither this passage nor Romans 11:25 teaches that Jerusalem is to have a further history after the so-called times of the Gentiles. Unless that idea is brought in from elsewhere there is no reason to think that the "until" indicates something earthly following for Jerusalem, a fiction about which Jesus says nothing. (See our chapter 10 for further explanation.)

John. Jesus' eschatology as reported by John gives us additional insight as to the resurrection (5:24-29; 6:39-40, 44-54; 11:1-44), as well as to the final judgement and eternal life.

In John 3 Jesus speaks of the nature of the kingdom. It is real but spiritual.

In John 14 He says:

> Let not your heart be troubled: ye believe in God, believe also in Me. In My Father's house are many mansions: if it were not so, I would have told you. I go to prepare a place for you. And if I go and prepare a place for you, I will come again, and receive you unto Myself; that where I am, there ye may be also (verses 1-3 KJV).

This simple, beautiful assurance need not be treated further eschatologically.

John 16 contains an explanation of the mission and work of the Holy Spirit to come, starting at Pentecost.

John 17 gives added insight into Christ's preexistence, preincarnate state, and the future glory.

John 18:36 again gives the nondispensational insight:

> Jesus answered, "My kingdom is not of this world. If My kingdom were of this world, then My servants would be fighting, that I might not be delivered up to the Jews; but as it is, My kingdom is not of this realm."

Acts. Except for His special appearance to Saul on the Damascus road and His speaking in the Book of Revelation, the first chapter of Acts contains the final words of Jesus.

In Acts 1:6 (RSV) the disciples ask, "Lord, will you at this time restore the kingdom to Israel?" On the surface this sounds as if an earthly millennium may have been expected by the apostles. Christ dismisses this, saying. "It is not for you to know times or epochs." They were to win converts from among Jews and Gentiles. Here is a helpful comment on the matter:

> The kingdom to be proclaimed under the terms of the Great Commission was "the kingdom of God." It was not to be Israelitish: it was to be world-embracing. This was the answer to the question as it related to Israel.[18]

Conclusion

The testimony of Jesus should be accepted as the truth, the whole truth, and nothing but the truth, full and final, for He is God. Both Testaments must agree in Him. None must take away from nor add to the perfect deposit of our Lord's teachings. Lawrence Thomas gives a wise caution in that regard:

> We are not to instruct people about future events which the Lord Jesus has not endorsed. Neither are we to set ourselves up as teachers of prophetical things which contradict His predictions (Matthew 12:36–42). A golden rule is: Where Christ is silent we ought to be silent also.
>
> . . . .
>
> It is the height of folly to run ahead of Him who is our Master. None of the Apostles added an opposing doctrine but did expand His.
>
> . . . .
>
> Be convinced, once and for all, that our Lord's method of interpretation should be the Christian's method. We must give Him the credit for

knowing the Old Testament better than we do. Everything He said about the Kingdom, the people who inherit it, and who were then entering it, comes direct from the Old Testament prophets. Christ is the Divine Interpreter.[19]

Such thoughts serve to reinforce the theme of this book. <u>Only the First and the Last knows the last things.</u>

One certainly shares Christian sentiments of good will toward godly people who love the Bible. No matter what system of prophetic interpretation they have been taught they are loved by our Lord Jesus Christ.

> It gives us no pleasure, but rather sorrow, to make these observations; but we feel that a devotion to Christ and His truth must take precedence over our deference to our fellow man, however highly regarded by ourselves and others.
>
> There was but one kingdom offered by our Lord Jesus Christ. He offers that kingdom to all who will enter into it today. . . . When he comes again He will call His people to Himself to "inherit the Kingdom prepared for you from the foundation of the world (Matthew 25:34)." That kingdom will not be Palestine, anymore than it will be Poland. . . . We cannot think of any proof that should be more conclusive in this respect than the silence of the New Testament regarding any such kingdom. The whole thought is foreign to the revelation given by Jesus Christ.[20]

Scripture cannot err nor contradict itself. Jesus taught that the world could end even in his disciples' lifetimes. Thus the "thousand years" of Revelation 20 did not mean the world could not end before A.D. 1,033 (1,000 years after Jesus). Nor can they be after he comes.

There is something pathetic about those who spiritualize away all reality and those who are blinded to the transcendent by hyperliteralism. Christ is coming, literally! He is the coming King. But "there are no literal thrones for Deity."[21]

There will not be an earthly political millennium during the course of history. Nowhere in the teachings of our Lord does one find a worldly reign of 1,000 years before or after his coming. The world ends when he comes. Multitudes will not be saved after his coming. The teachings of Jesus most emphatically cancel any possibility of salvation for even one soul after his coming.

<u>As he comes, resurrection occurs, the saved are caught away, raptured, as the universe ends in new creation. Judgment ensues. Eternal destinies follow. "When He comes *eternity* comes."</u>[22]

23

CHAPTER 2

Things to Come
and the Old Testament

"WHILE THE EARTH REMAINS, seedtime and harvest, and cold and heat, and summer and winter, and day and night shall not cease" (Genesis 8:22). This was God's first indication that the days of the earth were numbered. But the means of its dissolution would not be by water.

> I establish My covenant with you; and all flesh shall never again be cut off by the waters of the flood, neither shall there again be a flood to destroy the earth (Genesis 9:11).

There would not be multiple destructions—only one. "Thus says the Lord of hosts, Once more in a little while, I am going to shake the heavens and the earth, the sea also and the dry land" (Haggai 2:6).

> His voice shook the earth then, but now He has promised, saying, "Yet once more I will shake not only the earth, but also the heaven." And this expression, "Yet once more," denotes the removing of those things which can be shaken, as of created things, in order that those things which cannot be shaken may remain. Therefore, since we receive a kingdom which cannot be shaken, let us show gratitude, by which we may offer to God an acceptable service with reverence and awe; for our God is a consuming fire (Hebrews 12:26-29).

Our procedure in this chapter will be first to treat prophecies pertaining to the physical end of the world and the refashioning of the universe for eternity. Then the study will turn to the agenda of history to that point, with attendant problems of interpretation.

The End and Thereafter

It was a dim conception, but under the Old Covenant there was hope beyond the grave. The repeated phrase, "he slept with his fathers," indicated survival beyond death. Moses, David, Solomon, Daniel, and others spoke of judgment and of books of life (examples: Psalm 23:6; Exodus 32:32-33; Ecclesiastes 11:9; 12:14; Daniel 7:10).

Hope of the resurrection, a term that inherently means resurrection of the body, was held under the Old Testament too, as seen from such passages as Daniel 12:2-3; Job 19:25-27; Psalms 17:15; 71:20-21; 73:24-26; Jeremiah 31:15-17; Isaiah 66:24; Hosea 13:14.

The "how" of the earth's end is to be by fire, as seen throughout holy Scripture. Old Testament references to that include:

> On the day of the Lord's wrath . . . all the earth will be devoured in the fire of His jealousy, for He will make a complete end, indeed a terrifying one, of all the inhabitants of the earth (Zephaniah 1:18).

> The Lord will execute judgment by fire and by His sword on all flesh, and those slain by the Lord will be many (Isaiah 66:15-16).

> Behold, the day of the Lord is coming, cruel, with fury and burning anger, to make the land a desolation; and He will exterminate its sinners from it. For the stars of heaven and their constellations will not flash forth their light; the sun will be dark when it rises, and the moon will not shed its light. Thus I will punish the world for its evil, and the wicked for their iniquity; . . . And the earth will be shaken from its place at the fury of the Lord of hosts in the day of His burning anger (Isaiah 13:9-13).

> And all the host of heaven will wear away, and the sky will be rolled up like a scroll (Isaiah 34:4).

> "Lift up your eyes to the sky, then look to the earth beneath; for the sky will vanish like smoke, and the earth will wear out like a garment, and its inhabitants will die in like manner; but my salvation shall be forever, and my righteousness shall not wane" (Isaiah 51:6).

This destruction of the universe would be followed by the endless ages of eternity as is seen by these sample passages from Isaiah:

> "For behold, I create new heavens and a new earth; and the former things shall not be remembered or come to mind" (Isaiah 65:17).

> "The new heavens and the new earth which I make will endure before me" (Isaiah 66:22).

In the Meantime

Here is where the headwaters divide between the schools of interpretation. Dispensationalism divides the Bible or God's administration into seven dispensations and eight covenants. According to that system, the present *dispensation* is grace, with the kingdom dispensation still to come; and the present *covenant* is the New, with the Palestinian and Davidic to be reestablished.

However, the Bible, or God's dealing revolves around but two dispensations, Law and Gospel. Also there are but two basic covenants, the Old and the New, and essentially they are but one—everything converging in Christ.

Abrahamic and Davidic considerations. Dispensationalism makes much of the so-called Abrahamic and Davidic covenants, the former as a land promise to Jews only, and the latter as the promise of a 1,000-year kingdom still future from now, with Christ reigning at Jerusalem.

Premies and dispies are misled in limiting *to Jews alone* the seed and the land inheritance! The promise was given Adam and Eve that [Christ] the seed of the woman [not of a man and woman] would bruise the serpent Satan's head, Genesis 3:15 - the Seed has mainly to do with deliverance, not land. To fulfill that promise, God chose a people to be separated unto a land (Palestine) that they might be the lineage to bring the promised Seed, Christ, into the world. This lineage continued from Adam and Eve through their son Seth unto Abraham. To Abraham repeatedly the promise was given, then to Abraham's son Isaac, then to Isaac's son Jacob. In these repeats it was made clear that the land would belong to the entire seed *which would include believers of all nations.*

> I will give unto you, and to your seed after you, the land of your sojournings, all the land of Canaan, for an everlasting possession; and I will be their God. (Genesis 17:8)

> The promises were made to Abraham and to his seed. The Scripture does not say "and to seeds," meaning many, but "and to your Seed," meaning one, who is Christ. (Galatians 3:16)

> Abraham's blessing came on Gentiles through Jesus Christ - If you are Christ's, you are Abraham's seed. (Galatians 3:14, 29)

The error of restricting the seed and land promise to Jews, deludes them, and angers Arabs. The writer recalls an experience on a tour of the

26

Holy Land. Our tour bus driver was a Christian Arab. Speaking of false prophecy teachers from America who come there to support Jewish claims on Palestine, he said: "What's the matter with them? Don't they know this land belongs to *all* of us?"

Asked whether U.S. policy toward Israel was based on Bible prophecy, past President Nixon replied that our policy toward Israel was based on humanitarian and strategic reasons, not on any views of Bible prophecy. U.S. Congresses past and present have been influenced by wrong interpretations of the Bible as to the Middle East and the world's future. World leaders too have been misled. God takes no side in such politics of the Old Covenant which is no more.

To be sure, Abraham was promised a Seed and land, but in realization these were to be greater than he could conceive. That Abraham understood these promises in that greater-than-earthly sense is seen, for example, in Hebrews 11:10: "For he looked forward to the city which has foundations, whose builder and maker is God," and with other heroes of the faith, he desired "a better country, that is, a heavenly one (verse 16)." All God's seed will inherit the new universe!

Even the bed rock "land" passages—Genesis 12:7; 13:15; 17:8— do not belong to earthly literalism, for they too say "forever" and "everlasting," not "1,000 years." And Jacob is told in Genesis 28:14 that the Seed (Christ, Galatians 3:16) would burst all boundaries of land and race. Moreover, the temporal aspects were fulfilled—Joshua 21:45 "Not one of all the good promises which the Lord had made to the house of Israel failed; all came to pass." (See also Lowry, our page 56.)

As for the Davidic kingdom, David wanted to build a temple, a house for the Lord. But through Nathan the Lord tells David of His own "house" plan (Note: A non-1000 year kingdom, a non-1000 year throne):

> The LORD also tells you He will build a house for you. When your time is up, and you lie down with your ancestors, I will give you a Descendant who will come from you, and I will establish His kingdom. He will build a temple for My name, and I will make the throne of His kingdom stand FOREVER. I will be His Father, and He will be My Son.... Your royal house will stand firm before Me FOREVER, and your throne will stand firm FOREVER (2 Samuel 7:11-16 WFB).

The eternal kingdom would not be founded by his own son, but by "one of your descendants after you . . . I will establish his kingdom," 1 Chronicles 17:11.

The Davidic kingdom promise was not forgotten; for example, "In the coronation ritual each king was hailed as the adopted 'son' of Yahweh...."[1] This helped keep alive popular hope in the certainty and unchanging nature of Davidic promise.

Since a mix of divine and human factors was involved, no wonder that such a passage as Psalm 89 has repeated parallel references to both *chesed* (mercy) and *berith* (covenant). Verses 30-36 especially will serve to confirm what has been said to now:

> If his children should forsake My law, and walk not in My judgments; if they should profane My ordinances, and not keep My commandments; I will visit their transgressions with a rod, and their sins with scourges. But My mercy I will not utterly remove from him, nor wrong My truth. Neither will I by any means profane My covenant; and I will not make void the things that proceed out of My lips. Once have I sworn by My holiness, that I will not lie to David. His seed shall endure for ever (LXX).

The division of the kingdoms of Israel and Judah, ending the unity achieved under David; the captivities and returns; the helpless, rudderless intertestamental period: all were refining fires to teach the hope of a better and enduring kingdom. So was the Lord Jesus Christ awaited. Many mistakenly awaited Him in a materialistic kingdom sense. But those who awaited Him in the heavenly, eternal sense understood His kingdom aright, as do those who properly await Him now. His kingdom is not of this world.

The fundamental misunderstanding of dispensational premillennialism regarding the land and kingdom promise has to do with type and duration. The true Israel's inheritance is not to be *Palestine* but the *new earth*. The kingdom is not to be limited to 1,000 years, ending with destruction. *Over and over again the contexts of the supposed millennial kingdom passages use the word "forever";* therefore they cannot be applied to a 1,000-year period. Such hopes are "little and perishable," said an early church father.

Contradictions abound in the system that looks for a physical millennium. And while the greater and enduring kingdom view is not problem-free, it is wise to choose the lesser difficulties.

Inconsistencies are everywhere in futurist millennialism. Isaiah chapter 2, for example, is alleged to be future from now, though it clearly is our Gospel era, ending with earth's demise. Verse 4 and Micah 4:3 identically prophecy that people "shall beat their swords into plowshares, and their spears into pruning hooks; nation will not lift up sword against nation, and never again will they learn war."

But that can apply only to the eternal kingdom of Christ, for the earthly millennial kingdom must end in the most fearful war of history, Gog and Magog II, no less! The only way out of this conundrum would be for the earthly kingdom adherents to explain, "Well, nations will never again *learn* war, that is, take schooling in war; they will have to fight the big one without military training."

Also, the parallel to Isaiah 2:1-4 is Micah 4:1-7. Micah shows that not a 1,000-year reign but the Lord's "FOREVER" reign is meant.

Likewise chapter 11 of Isaiah is claimed by premies and dispies to speak of a time after Christ's return; yet the first verse makes plain that Christ's *first* advent is meant-the Branch growing out of Jesse's stem (David's father), with righteousness as his belt-"the Lord our righteousness"-compare 1 Corinthians 1:30 as one of many New Testament passages declaring that Christ is our righteousness.

Isaiah 11:6-10 pictures the gracious influence that the Prince of Peace has had now and forever: "The wolf will dwell with the lamb, and the leopard will lie down with the kid, and the calf and the young lion together; and a little boy will lead them . . ." Verse 10 repeats: "the root of Jesse"-an Ensign to whom the Gentiles also shall seek.

Verses 11-16 tell of a "second recovery" of the "remnant" (Isaiah 59:20; Romans 9-11). The first recovery was from Egypt; the second was not only from Assyria and Babylonia, but from all nations by the Gospel, as has been going on since Christ's first advent. So today, (verses 11, 16) Christian Jews and Christian Gentiles in joy travel the "highway for the remnant of his people"; in Isaiah 35:8-10 it is holiness highway" for "the ransomed of the Lord" with "EVERLASTING joy."

Daniel 9:24-27 is the answer to Daniel's prayer in Babylon seeking God for restoration of Israel from captivity. From the prophecy of Jeremiah (25:11; 29:10), Daniel saw that the exile would last 70 years till their return "from all the nations (29:14)" to Palestine. This was fulfilled on schedule starting 538 B.C. But in prophecies of the "latter days" (i.e. times of Messiah), Moses, angel Gabriel here, and our Lord, foretold that the unbelieving Jewish nation would be left desolate to world's end, except for the *seed*, the saved *remnant*.

Literally the opening of verse 24 would be rendered, "seventy sevens." The clue to correct understanding of the vision was within the grasp of a familiar defender of dispensationalism:

The Hebrew word is *shabua,* which means literally a "seven" and it would be well to read the passage thus, dropping for a moment the word "week" which to the English ear always means a week of days. Thus the twenty-fourth verse of Daniel's ninth chapter simply asserts that "seventy sevens are determined."[2]

In the splendid commentary by Edward J. Young this fact of "seventy sevens" is correctly handled–not "seventy weeks (of years)," as in most translations, but "seventy sevens." The 70th seven should be thought of as the entire Christian era, of undetermined length, between Christ's first and final advents. The extent of the 70th seven necessarily is unknown if the time of the final advent was to be unknown. Thus Christ's coming has been ever "at hand" though seemingly long delayed.[3]

One senses the genius of the Holy Spirit in conceiving of these "seventy sevens." A misunderstanding of them allows for the "gap" or "parenthesis" theory, that our church age was unforseen and runs between the 69th and 70th weeks of years. The 70th is said to be yet future! The dispensationalists say it cannot begin until the church is gone and a ten-nation confederacy emerges (toes of the image in Daniel 2) as a revived Roman empire; embarrassingly in late 20th century their 10-nation European Common Market sprouted into the 12-toed European Community, and on to the European Union. Undaunted, they hold that the feet and toes of the Daniel 2 image will reappear as the gap ends, a gap which has widened to many centuries! The Antichrist of dispensationalism arises out of this revived Roman empire and becomes world dictator, first from Rome, then from Jerusalem, Lindsey says.

Here is the sense (but last sentence "midst" for "half"):

In response to his prayer, Gabriel announces to Daniel that a period of sevens—the exact length of the seven is not stated—in fact, seventy of them, has been decreed for the purpose of accomplishing the Messianic work. . . .

This period is divided into two. The first period of seven sevens is evidently intended to include the time from the first year of Cyrus to the completion of the work of Ezra and Nehemiah, and the second that from the completion of the work of Ezra and Nehemiah unto the first advent of Christ . . .

After the expiration of these two periods, two events are to occur. Whether or not these two events fall within the 70th seven is not immediately stated. One of them is the death of the Messiah and the other follows as a consequent, the destruction of Jerusalem and the Temple by the Roman armies of Titus.

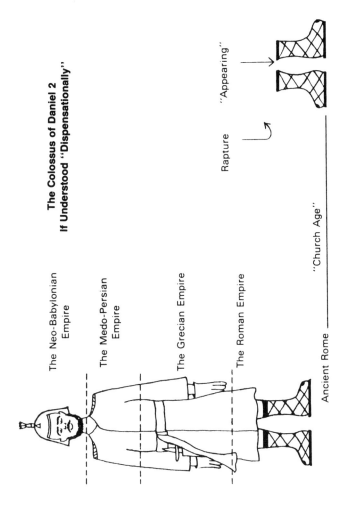

The Colossus of Daniel 2
If Understood "Dispensationally"

The Neo-Babylonian Empire

The Medo-Persian Empire

The Grecian Empire

The Roman Empire

Ancient Rome

"Church Age"

Rapture

"Appearing"

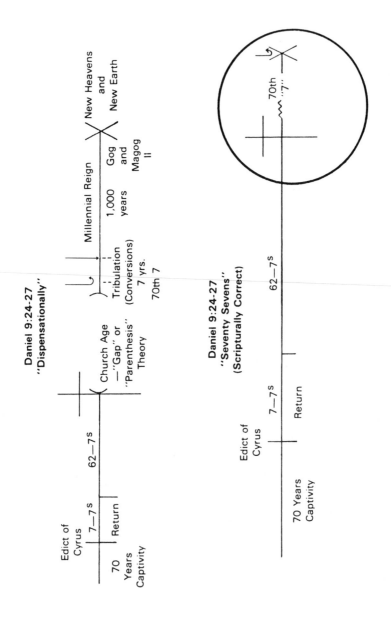

Daniel 9:24-27
"Dispensationally"

Edict of Cyrus

70 Years Captivity

7—7$

Return

62—7$

Church Age —"Gap" or "Parenthesis" Theory

Tribulation (Conversions) 7 yrs. 70th 7

Millennial Reign

1,000 years

Gog and Magog II

New Heavens and New Earth

Daniel 9:24-27
"Seventy Sevens"
(Scripturally Correct)

Edict of Cyrus

70 Years Captivity

7—7$

Return

62—7$

70th "7"

32

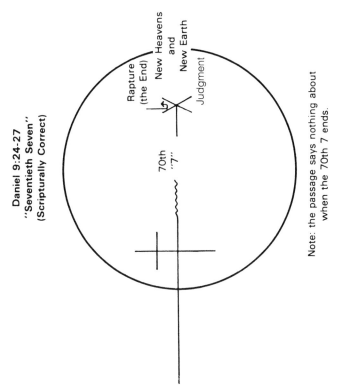

Daniel 9:24-27
"Seventieth Seven"
(Scripturally Correct)

Rapture
(the End)

New Heavens
and
New Earth

Judgment

70th
"7"

ETERNITY

Note: the passage says nothing about
when the 70th 7 ends.

33

For the period of the 70th seven the Messiah causes a covenant to prevail for many, and in the half of this seven by His death He causes the Jewish sacrifices and oblation to cease.[4]

Daniel 9:24-27 prophesied the restoration of Jerusalem, the coming of Messiah and his work of redemption, the destruction of Jerusalem and ending of the old covenant for its transition into the new one. Verse 24 stands wondrously fulfilled: *to finish the transgression,* i.e., to break its power, to bruise the head of the serpent (Genesis 3:15), "It is finished," Christ announced from the cross; *to make an end of sins* i.e. to wash them away in his blood so they shall not condemn us, and that where sin reigned unto death, grace might reign unto life; *to make reconciliation for iniquity,* i.e. chapter 53 of Isaiah explains this as to how "we were reconciled to God by the death of his Son (Romans 5:10)"; *to bring in everlasting righteousness* i.e. here as in the former, one might quote much of the New Testament and Old, "the Lord our righteousness," "Christ Jesus, who of God is made unto us wisdom, and righteousness, and sanctification, and redemption (1 Corinthians 1:30)," "one sacrifice for sins forever (Hebrews 10:12)"; *to seal up the vision and prophecy,* i.e. to seal up, to complete the present vision, accomplishing it and all things written in the law, the prophets, and the psalms, concerning the Messiah, which were fulfilled in him, the sure Word, God's last word to this world (Hebrews 1:1-2); *and to anoint the most holy,* i.e. Christ (means "anointed"; Luke 4:18 et al.), as well as his church, God's temple, the new and living way into the holiest by Jesus' blood.

The foregoing is so plain, yet a dispensationalist president of a theological seminary wrote of the foregoing that "The fulfillment of the tremendous events in verse 24 cannot be found anywhere in known history." How then *will* they be?! Dispies restrict the prophecy to Jewish people in future, as they do their Abrahamic and Davidic covenants, whereas "all nations" are intended and the human race included in "The Lamb of God who takes away the sin of the world."

To dispensationalism, verse 27, the 70th 7, is future (supposedly Revelation 4-19); their "he" is Antichrist with a false covenant. To the historic faith, the "He" is Christ, who ended sacrifice by the New Covenant which, from Calvary on, He has "confirmed with many!"

Ezekiel 37-39. No wonder these chapters have been camouflage for the view which perpetuates a national Israel and Palestine forever! The language of the book of Ezekiel, acknowledged by all to be more difficult, was directed originally to a dispossessed people who needed strong encouragement. However, Professor Patrick Fairbairn, in a work called *Ezekiel's Temple,* wrote:

> It defies all attempts to bring it within the bounds of the real (earthly). . . . an inescapable obstacle to their literalism. It is an incontrovertible evidence that the prophet had something else in his eye than the masonry stone and lime erections, and was labouring with conceptions which could only find their embodiment in the high realities of God's eternal kingdom. We regard the vast extent of the sacred area as a symbol of the vast enlargement that was to be given to the kingdom of God in the times of the Messiah.[5]

While the nonearthly kingdom viewpoint is hard pressed to adapt Ezekiel's strong language to the higher and greater kingdom of the Messiah, the earthly kingdom exponents are driven even harder to the wall. First (to be absolutely literal to both the "north" and the "four corners" descriptions) they must differentiate between the Gogs and Magogs of Ezekiel and Revelation, the former before the millennium, the latter after it. Other absurd opinions are necessitated, as in the following examples in *A Premillennial Problem,* by the late Dr. J. C. L. Carson of Coleraine, Ireland:

> Mede, the learned Premillennarian, . . . is able to inform us that the earth shall not be totally consumed, as America and Australia must of necessity be preserved from the general conflagration, in order to furnish the armies of Gog and Magog. . . . I must ask my readers what they think of a system which requires for its support to imagine that the glorified saints of heaven, and the damned in hell, are all to be brought up on the new and renovated earth, under the leadership of Christ and the Devil, for the purpose of fighting a really literal and corporeal battle. . . . We are disposed to laugh at the child, but a similar case crops up in the Premillennarian system, where the learned Dr. Burnet accounts for the armies of Gog and Magog by supposing that a new race of men "will be generated from the slime of the earth, and the heat of the sun."[6]

The proper understanding of Ezekiel 37-39 is aided greatly by bearing in mind Ezekiel's perspective. The "former years" refer to the time during or *before* the Babylonian captivity; the "latter years" to the time *after* it. It is of further help to remember that historically the chief battle was with Antiochus Epiphanes (Ezekiel 38-39). Chapters 40-48 are best understood as picturing the more glorious realities of the New

Covenant age, couched, however, in the language of the Old Covenant people.

> ... The basic meaning of the Book of Ezekiel will not elude the reader if he keeps in mind that God's glory and His great acts of judgment and salvation are portrayed in symbolic language and form. What Ezekiel sees in visions, describes in allegories, and acts out in a manner resembling charades, is designed to contribute to the assurance that God is carrying forward His plan of salvation for all men that He initiated in His covenant with Israel centuries ago. Purified by God's judgment in the Babylonian exile, Israel will again become the bearer of the promises to be fulfilled in the New Covenant and to the end of time. All of this Ezekiel sees in prophetic perspective, in which scenes of the immediate and of the distant future are at times superimposed on the same picture of the coming and enduring Kingdom of God.[7]

Zechariah 12-14. Zechariah's wondrous prophetic symbols, like Ezekiel's, provide fertile soil for interpretations hard to disprove.

It should be observed that, as is common in Old Testament prophecies, the details are not necessarily in chronological sequence. For instance, Zechariah 12:10 is cited by the apostle John as fulfilled at the crucifixion (looking on the pierced one)—not during a post-rapture tribulation period (see John 19:36-37); Zechariah 13:7 is cited by our Lord as having been fulfilled in his Gethsemane arrest the night before (see Matthew 26:31).

Whatever is made of Zechariah 14:6-11, it is clear that it speaks not of a physical millennium but of the Gospel era idealized, which issues in heaven: "There shall be neither cold nor frost.... there shall be continuous day.... Living waters shall flow out from Jerusalem.... the Lord will become king over all the earth.... the whole land shall be turned into a plain.... But Jerusalem shall remain aloft upon its site . . . there shall be no more curse" (Zechariah 14:6-11 RSV). This pictures new heavens and earth as in Revelation 21-22. "Continuous day" does not fit 1,000 years in our solar system.

A special word to those who fear to spiritualize: when the context or the literal sense would show contradiction, it is valid and safe to take something figuratively so long as it is understood to picture realities, realities which are greater. Accordingly, Zechariah 14:4 speaks of something greater than a physical split of the Mount of Olives. On the east side of Jerusalem it now rises from the valley of the Kidron to a height of some 600 feet. Zechariah 14:4 states:

In that day His feet will stand on the Mount of Olives, which is in front of Jerusalem on the east; and the Mount of Olives will be split in its middle from east to west by a very large valley, so that half of the mountain will move toward the north and the other half toward the south.

As a Gospel valley of escape for the remnant, 14:1-5 means:

The Lord Jesus Christ has already stood upon the Mount of Olives, and from its brow He looked down upon the city which represented the Hebrew nation. That nation fell into two parts at His coming.[8]

If Zechariah 14 spoke of a millennium, how contradictory (as also when Ezekiel's prophecies are made memorials) to have the perfect sacrifice, our Savior, reintroduce Old Testament sacrifices and feasts which He ended forever! Animal sacrifices never did and never will take away sins, Hebrews 10:4.

Proper Prophetic Perspective: In seeing how Old Testament prophecy is fulfilled, one must keep in mind that the last days are not future from us but began in the first century A.D.— "this is that which was spoken by the prophet Joel, 'And it shall come to pass in the last days . . .' (Acts 2:16-17)"; God "has in these last days spoken to us by his Son (Hebrews 1:2)." Thus the last days have been going on for all of A.D. One must keep in mind also the *whole* of Scripture, the analogy or harmony of faith. Interpretations must be rejected which violate it. For example, where two views may seem plausible, that one is correct which conforms to the absolutes such as: one gospel, one kingdom, one people of God, one time of salvation, one return of Christ, one physical resurrection, one judgment day for all.

Much mischief has come via persons who stray from those absolutes. It is said that the Church once groaned and awoke to find itself Arian (4th century A.D.). That error was hard to overcome. How tragic that much of the Church today is awaking to find itself Scofieldic! Many other Bible versions now have that dispensational premillennial system of headings and notes. To avoid buying them, check out Revelation 20.

To sum up, speaking of wrong interpretations which imagine a millennium that is future from us, Theodore Engelder in *Popular Symbolics*, wrote: "It is preposterous in its main contention, by which the significance of the great body of Old Testament prophecy (pointing to the Church and the New Covenant) should be transferred to a period following the second advent of Christ."

CHAPTER 3

The Apostolic Writings
on Things to Come

The apostles preached the same message to Jew and Gentile, "solemnly testifying to both Jews and Greeks of repentance toward God and faith in our Lord Jesus Christ" (Acts 20:21). The Holy Spirit dealt with both alike—see for example Acts 10:34-47; also Romans 1:16.

The progression of the kingdom into the church, composed of saved Gentiles and Jews whose blindness is removed, becoming God's worldwide "temple of living stones" (Ephesians 2:11-21; 1 Peter 2:5), is a Bible fact fully supported, as in Acts 15:13-18:

> . . . James replied, "Brethren, listen to me. Simon has related how God first visited the Gentiles, to take out of them a people for His name. And with this the words of the prophets agree, as it is written, 'After this I will return, and I will rebuild the tabernacle of David, which has fallen; I will rebuild its ruins, and I will set it up, that the rest of men may seek the Lord, and all the Gentiles who are called by My name, says the Lord, who has made these things known from of old.'"

James sums up "the words of the prophets" such as Isaiah 11:10 and Amos 9:11-12. Based on the poor translation "I will return" instead of "I will *turn* again," Scofield says Acts 15:16 "dispensationally is the most important passage in the N.T." (SRB p.1169), as if it referred to the second advent![1] To dispies, "After this" means rebuilding the Jewish kingdom after *Christ's* "return." But see what precedes in the Amos reference: God vows to sift Israel by Assyrian captivity, but later to "turn" from curse to blessing, which He did. And "In that day" would come Messiah's birth as David's Son to rebuild worldwide as He has! Yet dispensationalism uses Acts 15:13-18 *against* James' point, which was that the prophecies of rebuilding pointed to the first advent, not the second; and not only to Jewry but to "the rest of men . . .the Gentiles" as at *present*, not after the rapture.

Peter's "first" report meant commencement of the rebuilding of

David's "fallen tent" into a vast dynasty and living temple (2 Samuel 7:11-16), namely the Spirit-empowered church, a kingdom which was to spread throughout the earth. It has! It started with the incarnation of the Second Person of the Trinity as David's Son (Allis, page 148).

> Acts 15:13-18 is a very important passage in this discussion.... James declares that this rebuilding of the tabernacle of David is now [was then] taking place in God's visiting the Gentiles to take out of them a people for His name.[2]

Note that today's myth of "Israel's coming glory" had no place in the apostles' discussion. The "After this" of Amos (785-740 B.C.) was future from Amos, not future from this present age. Christ has built the prophesied universal kingdom of elect Jews and Gentiles.

The apostles say Jesus is reigning now. "They will quote the prophets to prove that Jesus Christ fulfills all the predictions."[3] At Christmas all sing: "He *rules* the world with truth and grace, and makes the nations prove the glories of his righteousness, and wonders of his love." On Pentecost the apostles proclaimed His reign had begun. Peter in Acts 2:29-31 has Christ on David's throne since the resurrection, principalities and powers subject to Him:

> Brethren, I may confidently say to you regarding the patriarch David that he both died and was buried, and his tomb is with us to this day. And so, because he was a prophet, and knew that God had sworn to him with an oath *to seat one of his descendants upon his throne, he looked ahead and spoke of the resurrection of the Christ,* that he was neither abandoned to Hades, nor did His flesh suffer decay.

Romans 9-10-11 are not future but ever operative, as a remnant of those with some Jewish genes are being grafted in again (Chapter 10).

1 Corinthians 15:23-24 "...Christ's coming, then the end"–no 1,000 years between, as some claim, adding to the Word of God.

> The word "then" in the phrase "then cometh the end" does not necessarily imply an interval between resurrection of the saints and "the end"; it is often used of immediate sequence. Many pre-millenarians admit this. Also let us notice that the word 'cometh' has no equivalent in the Greek, so that the phrase is just "then the end."[4]

The following four passages are of great significance for a study of Christ's coming: 1 Thessalonians 5:1-4; 2 Thessalonians 1:6-10; 1 Peter 4:7; and 2 Peter 3: 10-12. (See chapter 9 for a detailed analysis.)

The Antichrist, the Great Tribulation, and Armageddon

Antichrist is a personification assumed meant in Daniel, a "mouth speaking great things" who would "magnify himself above all," and in 2 Thessalonians 2: 1-12, the man of sin, lawless, usurping God's place in His temple, with Satan's power, signs and wonders of falsehood, deceit of unrighteousness, working of error. Only Apostle John uses the term antichrist, 1 John 2:18-24, an opponent or substitute, that does not acknowledge Jesus Christ come in flesh (1 John 4:3; 2 John 7), denies that Jesus is the Christ . . . denies the Father and the Son (1 John 2:22). Supplanting of Christ as vicar or by false confession has been seen as antichrist in denying direct access to God's saving gospel. Dangers abound. Dispensationalism makes this a world ruler after the rapture, thus keeping people from seeing that it itself is part of the present deception! Antichrist and other matters necessarily retain an element of wonder until the final, awesome moment of Christ's coming.

The Great Tribulation is this life. Our Lord has made that clear in John 16:33 and elsewhere. At the same time, He speaks of two periods when the manner of this tribulation would be unique: (1) In the destruction of Jerusalem under Titus in A.D. 70., in which, in the words of Josephus, "eleven hundred thousand," that is, 1,100,000, perished. It is reported that Titus, the Roman general, surveying the valleys below the walls of Jerusalem and seeing them full of bodies that had been cast down because of the stench, with thick putrefaction running about them, groaned, and called God to witness that this was not his doing. (2) In the time before the end. Whereas unparalleled suffering marked A.D. 70, unparalleled deception of every kind, even of the elect (Matthew 24; Revelation 20) mark these perilous times, as in the days of Noah and of Lot, plus seducing spirits, Satanic doctrines, apostasy, falling away; multiplied wickedness midst business as usual.

The Battle of Armageddon (Revelation 16) is not a battle between nations, but between God and evil powers—God's retributive "true and righteous" judgments. He gathers all evil in symbol at Har-Magedon (Mt. Megiddo, near Nazareth, where once from the heavens the stars in their courses fought against Sisera, Judges 5:19-20; the site also of other bloody contests). The mightiest earthquake brings the fall of the cities of the nations; the great city, Babylon of old, "comes in remembrance before God, to give unto her the cup of the wine of the fierceness of his wrath"; as in chapter six, the mountains and islands flee away. It is as climaxed in all six visions (chart, page 42).

There is NO SECRET COMING OF CHRIST AND REMOVAL OF THE CHURCH at Revelation 4:1. Dispensationalism ADDS this to the Bible. Chapter 20 is the chief argument between the historic faith and premillennialism as well as dispensationalism. It is treated in Chapter 5 herein.

The Book of Revelation—Parallel Visions

The most important clue to interpreting the Book of Revelation correctly is its use of different visions covering the same period, namely the New Testament era. It is well said in a convincing and widely used interpretive work on the last book of the Bible:

> There is, in the main, an adoption of what has been called the synchronistic or parallelistic system of interpretation. That system is (and deserves to be) gaining the approval of orthodox scholars.[5]

Said system is required *especially* when the book is interpreted more literally. In language much like that of Christ in Matthew 24:29, and of Peter in Acts 2:19-20, the Revelation reaches the first of a half dozen climaxes which sound like the end of earthly life and the present universe. One may wish to compare these six views of the End in 6:12–17; 11:15-19; 14:14-16, 19-20; 16:15-21; 19:11-21; and 20:11-15. It is particularly plain that repetition history is demanded by the following examples (compare also chapter 12 herein).

". . . the sun became black . . . moon became as blood; and the STARS of heaven fell unto the earth . . . and the heaven departed . . . and *every mountain and island were moved out of their places* (6:12-14 KJV); *"And every island fled away, and the mountains were not found"* (16:20 KJV). Note that an alternate translation of "moved out" in chapter 6 is "removed." The point is this: if the heavens depart and the universe disintegrates with all mountains and islands removed in 6:14, how in 16:20 can they again flee away, also STARS be back again in 8:12 and 12:4? Parallel visions are the answer. Further, understanding 6:12-14 literally, earth cannot survive when the stars, which include our sun, approach, let alone impact into earth—our earth instantly would be incinerated and explode. Dispieism here must spiritualize, "take away" from God's Word; for in Revelation 4-19 or 6-19 (its 7-year tribulation, i.e. 70th "week" of Daniel; and "time of Jacob's trouble—Jeremiah 30:7"—fulfilled in past!) it cannot allow the End and Refashioning of the universe, since that spoils its 1,000 year secular kingdom in chapter 20, and its carnal Palestine-forever.

41

Schematic of the Book of Revelation

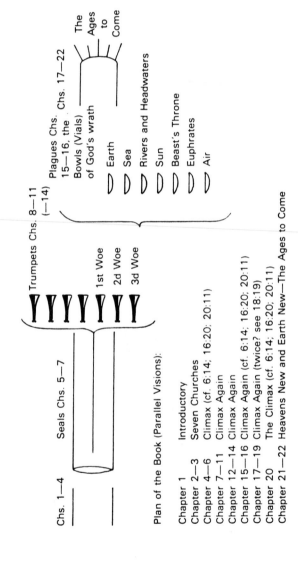

Chs. 1—4

Seals Chs. 5—7

Trumpets Chs. 8—11 (—14)

Plagues Chs. Chs. 17—22
15—16, the
Bowls (Vials)
of God's wrath

The
Ages
to
Come

1st Woe
2d Woe
3d Woe

Earth
Sea
Rivers and Headwaters
Sun
Beast's Throne
Euphrates
Air

Plan of the Book (Parallel Visions):

Chapter 1   Introductory
Chapter 2—3   Seven Churches
Chapter 4—6   Climax (cf. 6:14; 16:20; 20:11)
Chapter 7—11   Climax Again
Chapter 12—14   Climax Again
Chapter 15—16   Climax Again (cf. 6:14; 16:20; 20:11)
Chapter 17—19   Climax Again (twice? see 18:19)
Chapter 20   The Climax (cf. 6:14; 16:20; 20:11)
Chapter 21—22   Heavens New and Earth New—The Ages to Come

Plan of the Book of Revelation:
Parallel Visions, Synchronous
as required by such examples
as: **Chapter 6:14**
   Chapter 16:20
   Chapter 20:11

New Heavens and Earth
Heaven, Hell, the
Ages to Come

Vision 7   Chs. 21—22

The Rapture
and End:
Judgment Day

Ch. 1
Chs. 2—3

Vision 1	Chs. 4—6
Vision 2	Chs. 7—11
Vision 3	Chs. 12—14
Vision 4	Chs. 15—16
Vision 5	Chs. 17—19
Vision 6	Chs. 20

Book of Revelation
Parallel Visions
Inter-Advent
Period

Chapters 4—6

Chapters 7—11 (:18)

Chapters 12—14

Chapters 15—16 (:20)

Chapters 17—19 (:20)

Chapter 20

Same general history
but from various
perspectives,
or for various
purposes and
emphases.

A fair-minded spokesman correctly observes: "In chapter 12, it is unmistakably clear that the passage looks back to the birth of the Messiah."[6] All such may see that chapter 19 ends with all left slain, leaving no one for chapter 20 which therefore must start over.

Repetition does not exclude a sort of deepening and completing progression in the visions. Terror builds, yet God is in control and has the last word.

The preceding charts give a general outline, though the division points are not always clear in John's visions.

> If more than once, when the end is nearly reached, the writer turns back to the beginning, he does this in order to gather up new views of life which could not be embraced by a single vision.[7]

The general principle of recapitulation certainly is valid. And it gives added weight to that validity, for instance, to find a reference such as that in William Hendriksen in *More Than Conquerors,* (pp. 258-259), who lists 21 writers who assert parallelism for a proper handling of the Book of Revelation.

A single word in the Revelation as elsewhere, can mean much for truth or for error. For example, the word "rule" as often translated, in 19:15 means in the original to "shepherd." For errorists "rule" points to a future 1,000 year benign reign of Jesus from Jerusalem. But that verse–"smite the nations/shepherd them with a rod of iron/fury and wrath"–points to immediate destruction, as Revelation 2:27 (read shepherd, not rule) and Psalm 2:9 (KJV "break") declare!

No answer is the full answer to such a marvelous gem as John's Revelation. Dionysius of Alexandria showed a commendable restraint with the Book of Revelation and its visions: "I have regarded them as too lofty to be comprehended by me."[8]

The following quotation may serve to summarize this chapter dealing with the apostolic writings on things to come.

> The well-known English Christian worker, Mr. Frank L. Carter, writes: "Having in mind the teaching of all the New Testament writings, I affirm that the notation of a future millennium is unapostolic. Paul, James, Jude, Peter and John, are silent about such a thing in their letters. Could this be so were the doctrine of the millennium a part of the Christian deposit?"[9]

Our study now moves to the church's understanding.

CHAPTER 4

How the Church Has Understood Things to Come

It is commonly assumed and said by premillennialists that the early church was premillennial. In this chapter that contention will be explored in the church fathers, creeds, the reformers, and confessional documents.

William E. Cox in a catalog of testimonies states:

> The great majority of the church fathers, reformers, commentators, and teachers of the Bible have been either amillennial or postmillenial.[1]

Even earlier, A.D. 81–96, in the closing days of the apostles, Jesus' relatives are recorded as follows:

> There were yet living of the family of our Lord, the grandchildren of Judas, called the brother of our Lord, according to the flesh. These were reported as being of the family of David, and were brought to Domitian, by the Evocatus. For this emperor was as much alarmed at the appearance of Christ as Herod. . . . When asked also, respecting Christ and his kingdom, what was its nature, and when and where it was to appear, they replied, "that it was not a temporal nor an earthly kingdom, but celestial and angelic; that it would appear at the end of the world, when coming in glory he would judge the quick and dead, and give to every one according to his works."[2]

The Testimony of the Church Fathers

By the fourth and fifth centuries the influence of millenarian follies, even by some of the church fathers, hardly existed in the Eastern Church, and was rapidly dying out in the West. Here reviewed are the views of the early fathers from apostolic times.

> An able authority, the late Rev. E. P. Cachemaille, M. A., Scholar of Gonville and Caius College, Cambridge, and Secretary of the South

American Missionary Society, writes: "In the writings of the Fathers there are a multitude of references to the prophecy of Daniel and St. John. They correctly grasped the general principle that the prophets foretold the whole course of the Churches' warfare from the first century to the second advent. None of the Fathers entertained the idea of the Apocalypse overleaping the interval up to the consummation. The Judaic symbols of Daniel and St. John were generally referred to the Church and worship. Julius Afrikanius, Clement of Alexandria, Tertullian, explain the Seventy Weeks of Daniel Nine and the foretold desolations as being fully accomplished at Christ's death and the subsequent desolations of Jerusalem. So also Eusebius who spoke of the prophecy as being fulfilled years ago. So also Athanasius.

There was but one dissentient, Hippolytus. But he could never produce one text in support of his notion, hence the Fathers ignored his swansong. The modern Judaisers likewise cannot show us one Scripture.[3]

The same writer adds later:

There is no trace of a terrestrial millennial reign of Christ in the writings of Polycarp, the two Clements, Hermes, Dionysius, Ignasius, Diognius, Afrikanius, Athanasius, Cyril, Jerome and many others. The early document, The Didache, is free of millennialism also. The indices to the Ante-Nicean Fathers show 'Millennium' twice only.

Papias took his millennium fable from the uninspired book of Baruch. Justin and Barnabas based their millennium on the days of creation.[4]

Similar observations are frequent in the writings of those attempting to refute the idea of an earthly millennial kingdom. Grier states:

In the first half of the second century there are really only two to whom we can point with any certainty as hold a future reign of Christ on earth for a thousand years—Papias and Justin Martyr. There was, of course, the heretic Cerinthus also.[5]

Eusebius, in his *Ecclesiastical History,* refers to Papias as a historian but as including

some other matters rather too fabulous. In these he says there would be a certain millennium after the resurrection, and that there would be a corporeal reign of Christ on this very earth; which things he appears to have imagined, as if they were authorized by the apostolic narrations, not understanding correctly those matters which they propounded mystically in their representations. For he was very limited in his compre-

46

hension, as is evident from his discourses, yet he was the cause why most of the ecclesiastical writers, urging the antiquity of the man, were carried away by a similar opinion; as, for instance, Irenaeus, or any other that adopted such sentiments.[6]

As for Justin Martyr's writings, preserved in *The Ante-Nicene Church Fathers,* they are inconsistent on the subject, as shown by comparing "The First Apology of Justin" and his "Dialogue with Trypho the Jew." At least it was a mild form of millennialism, with believers simply living in Jerusalem for 1,000 years preceding "the eternal resurrection and judgment of all men."

Papias and Justin, then, are the only two of all the writers in the first sixty years of the second century who may with any certainty be called premillenarians. . . . Others definitely by their statements exclude premillenarianism. The first two volumes of the Fathers in the Ante-Nicene Library contain 950 pages, but the indices give only two references under the word 'millennium'; these two are to the statements of Papias and Justin.[7]

Let us pass from the Apostolic Fathers to the Old Catholic Church (A.D. 150–250). . . . The Apostles' Creed in its earlier forms comes to us from this time, and, according to it, there is no corporeal advent of Christ upon earth after His ascension on high, until He leaves 'from thence' to the last Judgment.[8]

The third century witnessed a very decided opposition to belief in an earthly millennium. Origen argued against it. His arguments at length gained a complete victory.[9]

Besides these, there are two works of his [Dionysius] *On the Promises.* The occasion of his writing this arose from Nepos, a bishop in Egypt, having taught, that the promises given to holy men in the Scriptures, should be understood more as the Jews understood them, and supposed that there would be a certain millennium of sensual luxury on this earth. Thinking, therefore, that he could establish his own opinion by the Revelation of John, he composed a book on this subject, with the title, *Refutation of the Allegorists.* This, therefore, was warmly opposed by Dionysius, in his work *On the Promises.*[10]

Lactansius was the only man of note in the fourth century who still held the system. Athanasius, the great defender of the doctrine of the deity of Christ against the Arians, speaks of Christ coming to judge the world; the good will then receive the heavenly kingdom and the evil will be cast into the eternal fire. This is his simple statement of the doctrine of the Lord's return.[11]

Augustine, who was one of the greatest men of the Christian Church of all time, lived A.D. 354–430. He at first adopted premillenarianism, but gave it up as "carnal." Augustine, says S. J. Case, laid the ghost of (pre-)millenarianism so effectively that for centuries the subject was practically ignored.[12]

In expounding Revelation Twenty, Augustine explained the binding of Satan as the fulfillment of the words of Jesus: "No man can enter into a strong man's house and spoil his goods unless he first binds the strong man." The reigning of the saints with Christ he looked upon as a present actuality.[13]

The Testimony of the Creeds

The Apostles' Creed in its earliest form dates from approximately A.D. 150. This and other creeds of the church uniformly look for only one return of Christ, bringing the end of the world. "From thence He shall come to judge the quick and the dead" (The Apostles' Creed). To think of the kingdom of Christ as yet future contradicts the creeds of Christendom, starting with the baptismal creeds of the second century; for Christ *did* set up a kingdom, they uniformly declare, and everyone born again is now in it.

The Nicene Creed (ca. A.D. 325):

[He] ascended into heaven, and sitteth on the right hand of the Father; and He shall come again with glory to judge both the quick and the dead; whose kingdom shall have no end.

The Athanasian Creed (ca. A.D. 500):

. . . . He ascended into heaven; He sitteth on the right hand of the Father, God Almighty; from whence He shall come to judge the quick and the dead. At whose coming all men shall rise again with their bodies and shall give an account of their own works. And they that have done good shall go into life everlasting; and they that have done evil, into everlasting fire. This is the catholic faith; which except a man believe faithfully and firmly, he cannot be saved.

Such declarations are all-inclusive and show no earthly kingdom intervening between the first century A.D. and the world's end.

The Testimony of the Reformers

When the Reformation came, millenarianism again appeared. It was an item in the belief of a wild and fierce sect of the Anabaptists.[14]

Luther spoke of those who were duped by the idea that before Judgment Day the Christians alone will possess the earth and that there will be no ungodly.[15]

Calvin is definitely on record as bitterly opposed to a wrong understanding of the millennium. Grier makes the following comment on Calvin's *Institutes,* Vol. 2, Book III, Chapter 25, Section 5:

> Calvin shows contempt for pre-millennial ideas when he says in the chapter on "The Final Resurrection" in his *Institutes,* that Satan has endeavored to corrupt the doctrine of the resurrection of the dead by various fictions, and adds: "Not to mention that he began to oppose it in the days of Paul, not long after arose the Millenarians, who limited the reign of Christ to a thousand years. Their fiction is too puerile to require or deserve refutation."[16]

Yet many today assume that Calvin taught premillennialism. He was a foe of it!

Anyone seeking additional statements of the Reformers can find them in such works as *Documents of the Christian Church,* selected and edited by Henry Bettenson, or in Philip Schaff's *The Creeds of Christendom.*

The Testimony of the Confessional Documents

To the three ecumenical creeds (Apostles', Nicene, and Anthanasian), may be added the doctrinal theology of the Eastern Orthodox Church, the Roman Catholic Church, and that of various Protestant churches. Selections from several of the latter are quoted here as representative of the array of communions that have adhered to what may be termed the traditional position on the millennium.

The Augsburg Confession (Lutheran), A.D. 1530:

> Also they (the Lutherans) teach that at the Consummation of the World Christ will appear for judgment, and will raise up all the dead; He will give to the godly and elect eternal life and everlasting joys, but ungodly men and the devils He will condemn to be tormented without end.
>
> They condemn the Anabaptists, who think that there will be an end to the punishments of condemned men and devils.
>
> They condemn also others, who are now spreading certain Jewish opinions, that before the resurrection of the dead the godly shall take possession of the kingdom of the world, the ungodly being everywhere suppressed (Article XVII).

The Belgic Confession (Reformed), A.D. 1561:

Finally, we believe, according to the Word of God, when the time appointed by the Lord (which is unknown to all creatures) is come, and the number of the elect complete, that our Lord Jesus Christ will come from heaven, corporally and visibly . . . (Article XXXVII).

The Westminster Confession of Faith (Church of England, Church of Scotland, Presbyterian), A.D. 1643:

At the last day, such as are found alive shall not die, but be changed; and all the dead shall be raised up with the self-same bodies, and none other, although with different qualities, which shall be united again to their souls forever. The bodies of the unjust shall, by the power of Christ, be raised to dishonour; the bodies of the just, by His Spirit, unto honor, and be made conformable to His own glorious body (Chapter XXII, II–III).

The New Hampshire Baptist Confession, A.D. 1833:

We believe that the end of the World is approaching; that at the last day Christ will descend from heaven, and raise the dead from the grave to final retribution; that a solemn separation will then take place . . . (Article XVIII).

Here is more from the Presbyterian heritage regarding the New Testament era:

In addition to our acquaintance with the Bible itself, it is profitable to consult the findings of those who have made a scholarly and exhaustive study of it. In this connection one thinks of the great Westminster Assembly of Divines, probably representing greater theological learning than any other Assembly before or since. This momentous conclave could not find in the Word of God the things which men profess to see so plainly in our day. The Westminster Assembly linked up the Lord's return with the general resurrection and judgment, but nowhere in their conclusions can one find a place for the interjection of one thousand years of earthly bliss. Their interpretation leaves room for only the amillennial eschatological position.[17]

In May 1944 the Southern Presbyterian Church in the United States adopted a report against dispensationalism.

The general tenor of our Lord's teaching and of the entire New Testament is that one should hold fast the original doctrine and be wary of latter day departures from it. The historic church, "the pillar and ground of truth" (1 Timothy 3:15, KJV), from its beginning has dealt with every conceivable form of new interpretation. A study of the best-known articles of faith will show that Orthodox, Roman Catholic, and major Protestant groups all conclude from Scripture a return of Christ only at the end of the world.

CHAPTER 5

Revelation 20 Rightly Understood

No one remains, for all not at the Marriage Supper are "slain," (19:21). So 20:1-10 goes back to Christ's binding of Satan (Matthew 12:29), to show here his doom. The thousand years must be symbolic, for the world's end was possible from Jesus on, and ends when He comes.

Revelation 20:1-10 and notably verse 4, says *nothing* about a coming to earth to reign. It is a heavenly reign of "souls" "with" Christ now, even as believers "reign in life *by* Jesus Christ (Romans 5:17)."

In comparison, Revelation 5:10 should be examined: "We shall reign over the earth." This need not mean bodily, nor "upon" the earth. It may be conducted from heaven. Nor is it said to be for 1,000 years. An Easter song runs: "He arose a Victor from the dark domain, And He lives forever with His saints to reign."

Satan Bound and Christ Reigning

The fact that it is hard to see how Satan is bound now, makes one an easy prey to error. Revelation 20 verses 3,8, speak only of restraint on his *deceiving* power. Furthermore, the Greek allows for a rendering of either "any longer" or "any further" (verse 3). That is to say, Satan's work of deceiving was greatly eclipsed at the first advent of Christ. Before that time, Satan had the whole world in his grasp except for a small number who waited for the consolation of Israel. What a difference today's billion! Christ came, bound (limited) Satan strongly, and has been taking Satan's plunder—Matthew 12:29, Augustine's proof passage on the binding of Satan.

The two most significant passages regarding the binding of Satan are not found in the Book of Revelation. The first reads:

> Angels who did not keep their own domain, but abandoned their proper abode, He has kept in eternal bonds under darkness for the judgment of the great day (Jude 6).

Satan of course is one of those fallen angels. Note the past tense: "has kept in eternal bonds." Satan has been in bonds ever since he fell. To say that he is not bound contradicts this clear statement. The second passage is 2 Peter 2:4:

> God did not spare angels when they sinned, but cast them into hell and committed them to pits of darkness, reserved for judgment.

Note again the past tense, also the words "hell" and "pits of darkness."

That binding as to Satan's deceiving arts was imposed specifically by Christ's crucifixion, resurrection, and ascension, when He "led captivity captive," Ephesians 4:8; Colossians 2:15; 1 Peter 3:22, all, Satan too, subjected to him. Revelation 20:2–3 Matthew Henry saw as:

> . . . a certain term of time, in which he should have much less power and the church much more peace than before. The power of Satan was broken in part by the setting up of the gospel kingdom in the world; it was further reduced by the empire's becoming Christian.[1]

In *Pilgrim's Progress,* John Bunyan has a character give the advice, "Stay in the middle of the path, for the lions are chained."

It is difficult to understand how Satan can be active and yet be "bound" (limited); but the same word is used of marriage! Moreover, Christ may allow more freedom to the inferior demons.

Not all evil is due to satanic activity, for man now is by nature sinful. Some need no tempting. That the devil is bound, therefore, is not to say all evil has ceased. If that being and his host were blotted out, the world still would be full of sinning.

Though limited or restrained as on a leash, Satan is a dangerous being within the scope of activity God allows him. Therefore we are warned: "Be of sober spirit, be on the alert. Your adversary, the devil, prowls about like a roaring lion, seeking someone to devour" (1 Peter 5:8).

Gog and Magog

What a perfect way of stating briefly the dark days prior to His coming at world's end. It is how our Lord taught. Satan is loosed, that is, given sway again. What a battle! It is spiritual, as with Armageddon. It is not nation vs. nation (verses 7-8), but nations vs. the church. This is shown by verse 9 when compared with Hebrews 12:22-23. These "saints" are not 1,000 year kingdom saints in physical Jerusalem, nor is Jesus said to be there as king. Verses 9-11, the instant End!

Judgment Day

Revelation 20:11-15 involves everyone. In addition to the living, the *dead* are there. "And (or Greek, *also*) I saw the dead—books were opened, another of life—and (or also) the dead were judged out of the books according to works—whoever was not found in the book of life was cast into the lake of fire." For "whoever," see Matthew 25:46.

> This is the preparation for the final judgment. Some interpreters are greatly interested in the time and place of judgment and theorize that there are several different and distinct judgments taught in the New Testament: the judgment of the nations to decide which nations enter the millennial kingdom (Matt. 25:31-40); the judgment of believers before the judgment seat of Christ in heaven to receive their rewards for what they have done in the body (2 Cor. 5:10); and the great white throne judgment of the present passage which is a judgment only of unbelievers. Such a scheme of eschatology cannot be proved but rests upon unsupported inferences. For instance, the final issue of the judgment of nations is not the millennial kingdom but is either eternal life or eternal punishment (Matt. 25:46).[5]

Exactly! Eternity has arrived! The sheep go into everlasting life, not 1,000 years of imperfection, a mix of sin and righteousness, ending in rebellion by many of the sheep! Also "my brethren (Matthew 25:40)" means Christians, not Jews. Further, the Bible as in Matthew 25:31-46, uniformly teaches one judgment at the last day for all humanity, dead and living, with every unconfessed thing coming out publicly, every idle word, wrong-doer exposed, wronged exonerated. To depart from this may mean loss of salvation (Athanasian Creed).

Were it not for Revelation 20's misunderstood millennium, post-, pre-, and premillennial dispensationalism would have nowhere to go with "literal" fulfillments except to 1) the Jewish return to the holy land "from all the nations (Jeremiah 29:14)" with rebuilding of the temple which happened via the edict of Cyrus, 538 B.C., 2) this Gospel age, or 3) heaven. Those who mislead and the misled should study such Scriptures using four classifications by the sainted Dr. Cecil Lowry: a) those that found their fulfillment under Zerubbabel, and in the centuries before Christ; b) those that will never be fulfilled, because God's conditions were never met; c) those that were fulfilled in the saved remnant of Jewry (Romans 11 :7) at the time of Christ and the Apostles, who came under the New Covenant; and d) those being fulfilled in New Covenant Israel (Philippians 3:3; Galatians 3:29).

The claim that the Abrahamic and Davidic covenants were unconditional is true only of the saved remnant-true for the elect seed, not for those of Israel who continue in unbelief. Furthermore, the issue is dead, for the literal 1,000 years envisioned would be too short and poor a bed for those glories which eye has not seen, nor heard, nor imagined, which God has prepared for those who love Him.

In summary, the millennium is Christ's inter-advent period of restraint on Satan until a final, brief release. It is the Gospel era. It is non-future, non-earthly, and of symbolic, unknowable length, for the possibility of the world's end has existed and been expected from apostolic times. The earthly golden era myth is not to be found even here in Revelation 20! The reader is urged to read Revelation 20:1-10 once again to discover the *absence* of an earthly reign of splendor therein, and here is the only place in the Bible where this thousand years is found. Its length is mystery, possibly extended, as with the when of Christ's coming. It omits the figure 1, unlike other thousands in the book. It represents unknown time prior to the end. It must not be made a tail to wag the dog, overturning all the Bible which says No to such a known time period *before* Christ comes, and No to *any* such time *after* He comes. "Thousand" can mean fulness (Psalm 50:10), 10 x 10 x 10, or God's time. It can be an extended period. Strange that those who futurize it and can stretch the *day* of the Lord or even an *hour* (John 5:28-29) into 1,007 years and more, nevertheless demand that the thousand years of Revelation 20 must mean just that, and in a book of so much symbolism! Inconsistency is the rule.

The following charts are included as clarifications of the Book of Revelation, especially of chapter 20. The second uses terms that vary among millenarian systems: the rapture, the appearing, and the end— these may be designated also as the rapture, the revelation, and the consummation.

**The Book of Revelation
in the Traditional View**

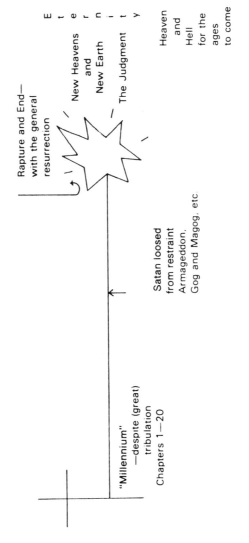

"Millennium"
—despite (great)
tribulation
Chapters 1—20

Satan loosed
from restraint
Armageddon.
Gog and Magog, etc.

Rapture and End—
with the general
resurrection

New Heavens
and
New Earth

The Judgment

Eternity

Heaven
and
Hell
for the
ages
to come

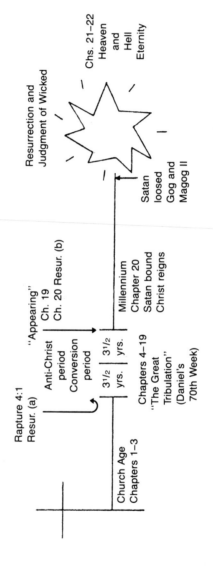

The Book of Revelation
in the Premillennial Dispensational View

Rapture 4:1
Resur. (a)

"Appearing"
Ch. 19
Ch. 20 Resur. (b)

Resurrection and
Judgment of Wicked

Chs. 21–22
Heaven
and
Hell
Eternity

Anti-Christ
period
Conversion
period

3½
yrs.

3½
yrs.

Chapters 4–19
"The Great
Tribulation"
(Daniel's
70th Week)

Millennium
Chapter 20
Satan bound
Christ reigns

Satan
loosed
Gog and
Magog II

Church Age
Chapters 1–3

58

CHAPTER 6

At Christ's Coming

It will be helpful to review what leads up to this momentous event. Outwardly, things will continue about as at present. The general signs spoken of by our Lord will become more intensified, but this has been happening and is almost imperceptible. Our Lord points to this situation in explaining that it will be business as usual, so to speak. There will be a general unawareness of the end; it will be unexpected.

> For this reason you be ready too; for the Son of Man is coming at an hour when you do not think He will (Matthew 24:44).

Meanwhile, the church will continue bearing witness to Christ until He comes. Marked apostasy increases as the end approaches; God removes restraint, loosing Satan in all fullness for "a little while" (Revelation 20:3). These are times of great trial for the people of God. The trial of Christian loyalty throughout history and especially near the end is symbolized by "666" (Revelation 13:18). Six, falling short of perfect seven, symbolically represents evil (Romans 3:23). Only God sees and knows whether His name (Revelation 14:1) or 666 marks us right now! Emperor worship in John's day, "Heil Hitler" then communism on to new isms in ours, exemplify the required submission: conform to survive! It was thus in that first century; it is ever so in marching to the world's drum—no one can buy or sell (Revelation 13:16-17) without the mark, conformity, on right hand (allegiance of body) or forehead (allegiance of mind)—subtle and dangerous for all.

Then in a moment, in the twinkling of an eye, Christ will come with clouds of heaven, attended by the holy angels and the saved who are now with Him. The resurrection will occur in that same moment as the saved soul is reunited with its gloriously resurrected body. These rise first as believers living on earth are changed, transformed instantly in body, and "caught up together with them in the clouds, to meet the Lord in the air (KJV)." ("Rapture" passages are Matthew 24:40-41; Luke 17:34-36; 1 Thessalonians 4:13-18; 1 Corinthians 15:51-52; and John 14:3.)

As this happens, the earth and universe will disintegrate with awesome destruction which those who are left must pass through as they are brought to judgment. In this same dissolution of the universe, a destruction by explosive fire and dissolving of the elements, there will occur also the refashioning which God has promised, resulting in the new heavens and new earth as the abode of righteousness.

In the same act of resurrection spoken of above, Christ will raise also the unsaved dead. Each soul presently in the preliminary hell will be reunited also with its raised body, but it will be a body of shame and contempt. Indescribable anguish that will never end begins for these, for whom all hope is lost. As in Dante's epic, the entrance to the place of the damned is posted with the solemn reminder:

"All hope abandon, ye who enter here!"

The great judgment now follows in this all-encompassing event, with the fixing of eternal destinies. The lost will be cast into hell "where their worm does not die, and the fire is not quenched" (Mark 9:43–48). The saved will be welcomed to new and glorious realms prepared for those who love God.

There is no place in all this for an earthly millennium after His coming. Yet the Scofield Bible footnotes speak of

. . . the good news that God purposes to set up on the earth, in fulfillment of the Davidic Covenant (2 Sam. 7:16, and refs.), a kingdom, political, spiritual, Israelitish, universal, over which God's Son, David's heir, shall be King, and which shall be, for one thousand years, the manifestation of the righteousness of God in human affairs. . . .[1]

Lindsey, by not literalizing some things and carnalizing others, says in that future 1,000 years all people of the earth will come annually ("feast of tabernacles" Zechariah 14) to worship Jesus at Jerusalem. Imagine, for example, problems of airline accommodations, lodging, traffic, seating in the temple, to name a few. No, such Scriptures speak in Old Testament figures of gospel-worship, the gospel-church. Yet today some hold that the kingdom "will finally be manifested, the consummation of all things visible on earth, the most splendid period of its history."[2] The issue is stated clearly as follows:

Will the coming of Christ terminate this present gospel age and be followed by the last judgment and the final state? Or, will it usher in another dispensation, the millennium, during which Christ will reign on earth and after which He will come to judge the world?[3]

60

A scholar and minister who once embraced and taught the dispensational view of things to come but then repudiated it, has written a counteracting description of what happens at Christ's return as eternity is ushered in—

We believe that the Second Coming of Christ will mark the end of this age and the beginning of the eternal one; We believe that the modern theory of a Secret Coming of our Lord, a Secret-Rapture of His Church, seven years before His Second Coming is a dangerous error and thoroughly unscriptural; We believe that there is but one future, bodily return of Christ, called His Second Coming, at which time the Church is Raptured; We believe that Christ's Second Coming will be as sudden and as unannounced as that of a thief in the night; We believe that at Christ's Coming the door of Salvation will be forever closed to sinners; We believe that on the day of His coming, on the Last Day of time, at the time of harvest, our divine, Lord Jesus Christ, our Great Prophet, Priest and King, shall descend from heaven corporally and visibly, in clouds of glory with a shout and with the voice of an Archangel, at which time there will be a General Resurrection of all the dead, of the just and that of the unjust; We believe that the righteous dead (whose bodies will have been reunited with their souls which will return from Heaven with their Lord) will rise first, and the living saints whose bodies will be suddenly changed (glorified), will be caught up together with them to meet the Lord in the air; We believe that Death will be destroyed at Christ's Coming; We believe that Christ is Coming the Second time to judge the living and the dead; We believe that at this General Judgment all apostate angels and all persons that have lived upon the earth shall appear at the Great White Throne Judgment to be judged by the most holy and righteous Judge—our Lord Jesus Christ; We believe that on that Day everyone, both believers and unbelievers, shall be judged according to their thoughts, words and deeds, and shall be rewarded according to the deeds done in their body, whether good or evil; We believe at that Day He shall say to the wicked, "Depart from me, ye cursed, into everlasting fire, prepared for the Devil and his angels"; We believe at that Day He shall say to the righteous, "Come, ye blessed of My Father, inherit the Kingdom prepared for you from the foundation of the world"; We believe in a place of eternal torment for the damned, and an eternal Kingdom of Glory for the redeemed; We believe that at Christ's Second Advent, according to Saint Peter (2 Pet. 3:10-14), the present heavens shall pass away with a great noise, and the elements shall melt with fervent heat, the earth also and the works that are therein shall be burned up; We believe that the teaching of God's Word is very clear as to the end of the world, and we, with Saint Peter and the Church of the ages, look, at the close of this age, for a "New Heaven and a New Earth, wherein dwelleth righteousness," not for a future thousand-year age of sin and imperfection mingled with righteousness (as do all premillennialists), a Millennial age which is supposed to consummate with the most fearful rebellion against God since man's creation.[4]

The same writer lists seven effects of Christ's coming:

1. Christ's coming shall mark the end of Christ's present mediatorial reign at God's right hand. Psalm 110:1; 1 Cor. 15:23–25.

2. Christ's coming will mark the end of the day of Salvation, of every sinner's chance to be saved. 2 Cor. 6:2; Phil 1:6; Matt. 25:10; Luke 13:25–28; 17:26–30; Matt. 13:37–43; 2 Thess. 1:7–10.

3. Christ's coming will bring the rapture of the Church, but destruction to the sinner. 1 Cor. 15:51, 52; 1 Thess. 4:16, 17; Luke 17:26–30; 2 Thess. 1:7–10; 2 Peter 3:7, 10, 11.

4. Christ's coming will bring the end of time—the end of this world. Matt. 13:37–43.

5. Christ's coming will bring the general resurrection of all men, and it will destroy death. Acts 24:15; John 5:28, 29; Rev. 1:7; John 6:39, 40, 44, 54; John 11:24; Matt. 12:41; 1 Cor. 15:25, 54, 55.

6. Christ's coming will bring the General Judgment of all mankind. Acts 17:31, 32; Matt. 16:27; Rev. 22:12; 2 Cor. 5:10, 11; Matt. 12:36; Luke 11:31, 32; Matt. 13:24, 30, 39–43; Matt. 25:31–46; Rev. 20:11–15.

7. Christ's coming will bring destruction to the present "heaven and earth," and will bring about a "new heaven and a new earth." Matt. 24:35; Heb. 1:10–12; 2 Pet. 3:7–15; 1 Cor. 13:10; 2 Pet. 3:18.[5]

There can be no doubt whatever about the *what* of the end. But the *when* is an important question also. The story is told that a Scottish teacher of the Gospel once asked a group of young ministerial students if they thought the Lord might come that very day. Each was asked in turn, and each answered in turn in this manner, "I think not." Whereupon the questioner said, "In such an hour as you think not, the Son of Man cometh."

CHAPTER 7

Second Chance: Error of Errors

". . . and the door was shut" (Matthew 25:10). The main point of Jesus' parable of the Ten Virgins is preparedness; its main lesson is that if one is unprepared at His coming it will be forever too late.

Only the boldest of the bold would dare to say that this parable applies mostly to a select period and people. The reader is referred to chapter 1 of this book for discussion regarding the error of differentiating between a "kingdom of God (Gentile)" and a "kingdom of heaven (Jewish)." Christ's "Be ready" is changed to "You need not be."

Any system which contradicts this *shut door principle* and which allows for even one conversion after the rapture has to be wrong and should be avoided as a fatal disease. This principle has ever been held with proper fear and no doubt kept many from embracing millennial systems which do violence to our Lord's repeated warnings against any idea of a second chance. But, as has been pointed out: "One of the worst features in the teaching of many pre-millenarians is a second chance."[1] It hurts to find those words confirmed in writings of good and godly Christians.

> To be sure, the chiliasts teach that there will be men and women saved after the gospel dispensation, just as there were people saved before the gospel age. . . . the Church will be complete when Christ returns, but, although no more will be added to the body of Christ, many more will be added to the multitude of the redeemed of God. . . . God's Word will be found on earth after the departure of the Church for heaven.[2]

By *second chance* in this discussion is not meant a repeated offer but an extension of the day of salvation. Christ spoke of returning only once at the end of the world. Therefore all systems must be scrapped which keep the door of salvation open after His one and only coming to judge the living and the dead. Gross error may sound reasonable:

The revising editor of the Scofield Bible, Mr. E. Schuyler English, wrote us: "Nowhere does the Scofield Bible teach a second chance. If I read my Bible aright, when Christ arrives He shall find many who had never heard the true Gospel and will then do so. This is not a second chance but a first chance."[3]

But *today* is the day of salvation. There will be no other.

A widely heard radio Bible teacher stated that the greatest moving of the Spirit of God will be after the church is taken away! Some premillennial teachers soften this objectionable aspect by saying that only Jews will have a second chance for salvation after Christ comes for the church; some say that Jews and certain Gentiles will have a second chance; still others make the second chance a wholesale opportunity with multitudes that no man can number being saved after Christ's return for the church. And really this latter view is more consistent with premillennialism for otherwise there could not be the spiritual and other millennial perfections.

In line with this, Ironside, a noted Bible teacher of the past, erroneously explains Revelation 7:13–14 as

> *the great ingathering* of the *coming* dispensation, when from all nations, and kindreds, and peoples, and tongues, a vast throng from all parts of the earth will be redeemed to God by the blood of the Lamb, and will enter into the earthly kingdom of our Lord. During the dark days of the great tribulation they will heed the testimony which will be carried to the ends of the earth by Jewish missionaries . . ."[4]

He echoes the Scofield Reference Bible system which teaches a second period of salvation after Christ's return, as on Acts 1:11: "To Israel, the return of the Lord" will "accomplish . . . her national regathering, *conversion,* and establishment in peace and power," and that "to the Gentile nations the return of Christ is predicted to bring the destruction of the present political world-system . . . followed by *world-wide Gentile conversion*" (italics added).

Many disturbing manifestations of this falsehood are cropping up. Books on how to be saved if one misses the rapture and how to survive during the tribulation are being marketed.

Songs such as, "I Wish We'd All Been Ready" and "The King Is Coming" tend to sow this dangerous idea of more time after Christ's coming—an open door to second chance teaching.

A 14-year-old reportedly told his preacher father something like this: "Dad, I'm not going to accept the Lord now. But I promise you if

I miss the rapture, I will accept Him then even if I have to have my head cut off."

Bulletin boards announce rapture topics such as "Resurrection—Don't Miss It."

A Bible lecturer on a university campus advised a large audience that if they should miss the rapture, all should fall down on their knees immediately because the great tribulation would be coming.

Bumper stickers pass along the idea. One reads: "In case of the RAPTURE this car will be unmanned."

At a local supermarket the writer one day was standing in a checker's line. The checker knew that the writer was a Gospel minister. Leaving the line momentarily, unnoticed by her, he picked up a forgotten item. Coming back he saw that she looked like death warmed over. "Oh!" she gasped. "Oh! I thought I missed the rapture!"

Damaging films are being shown such as "Thief in the Night." It concocts a story of a young couple—he is saved and so disappears at the rapture, but she is left. Refusing to join the 666 peace coalition, she at last commits suicide. Audience applause was unreal, appalling—a sort of erroneous western. One is left to wonder, was she saved by suicide? If not, she should have played it smart for three and a half years so as to get in on the mass conversion supposedly coming. The film ostensibly was based on 1 Thessalonians 5:1-3.

> Now as to the times and the epochs, brethren, you have no need of anything to be written to you. For you yourselves know full well that the day of the Lord will come just like a thief in the night. While they are saying, "Peace and safety!" then destruction will come upon them suddenly like birth pangs upon a woman with child; and they shall not escape.

But in the film's false doctrinal system, there *was* no destruction, no end. Moreover they *did* escape.

Offered now are guides for survival to leave behind for unsaved people, so they can still reach heaven the hard way if they miss the rapture. A note is left, informing them where to find the cassette. It tells them: "You can still be saved . . . you can attain salvation and join your loved ones in heaven later," then gives instructions. With denominational approval, a 2,000-member church in southern California has changed its bylaws to provide for continued leadership if its officers suddenly are taken to heaven. Error compounds. In still another example, efforts have been launched to stockpile Bibles in hidden, protective capsules for those who are left on earth after the rapture so that they may make it yet as "tribulation" saints.

Satan loves, furthers, and prospers any doctrine which hints to people that there may be a second chance. Such an assurance fosters a wait-and-see attitude.

This false teaching is bound to work great harm. It has and it will. The pages of Christian history contain many such examples. Years ago a great stir was caused by an erroneous expectation of the rapture. Newspapers were ready, just in case, with a headline that could be set on the presses in twenty minutes: "MILLIONS DISAPPEAR." When nothing happened, a credibility gap followed. It was a great victory for the devil. It confused some believers who turned away. It turned off much of the church from an interest in prophecy. It caused people in general to ignore Christianity.

CHAPTER 8

More than One Return, Resurrection, Judgment?

That question does not arise from the Bible unless one (a) departs from the historic faith by making the "first" resurrection of Revelation 20 a *physical* resurrection, and (b) allows the Old Testament to overrule the New which clarifies and modulates the Old.

The mistake of (a) above, may be called dog-wagging, letting the tail wag the dog. This wrecks the order of Scripture; for the literal or natural understanding of all the Bible is a single return, a single physical resurrection, and a single judgment. The mistake of (b) above is in having the Old Testament interpret the New.

Once this is done, a system is born—premillennialism—a coming of Christ with a Rapture before a thousand year millennium. So now *three* returns are required for the system: a first at the Rapture; a second at the Appearing (either yoyo-like, almost immediately, or seven years later as in the dispensational system); and, to fit all the rest of the Bible, a third return following the thousand years.

The "taken" and "left" of Matthew 24:39–43 and Luke 17:33–37 does not mean that the world goes on despite Christ's coming, but simply that at Christ's coming, human beings will be separated, the saved taken and the lost left to pass through the awesome destruction of the earth and heavens and be brought into the Judgment.

Can you see, reader, why the pre- and dispie systems must be wrong? They require not only extra returns/resurrections/judgments, but (in dispieism) extra captivities, extra destructions of Jerusalem, extra ages, and so on, twisting Holy Scripture at every turn.

Some passages speak of Christ's return as it relates to the saved without saying what happens with the lost. That is to be expected, for the Bible is written to believers primarily. Not mentioning both gives opportunity for error to creep in with the interpretation that there will be a separate return for the saved instead of one return involving saved and lost, as our Lord teaches, also all the Bible.

A coming, secret or other, before His final coming is NOWHERE FOUND in the Bible. Rather, it will be as was his departure—on the clouds of heaven with power and great glory. This we now await. At least seven different Scripture passages from Daniel to Revelation affirm that He is coming with clouds and that every eye will see Him, (Daniel 7:13; Matthew 24:30–31; Luke 21:27; Mark 14:62; Acts 1:11; Revelation 1:7; 14:14). By the miracle of an instantaneous resurrection and the momentary dissolution of the heavens and the earth, people in all ages and lands, from Adam to the last person born, will see His coming.

Some passages speak of physical resurrection as it relates to the saved without saying what happens with the lost. Again, this does not mean separate resurrections for saved and lost. *There are not two physical resurrections, but two classes of the resurrected!*

The common New Testament teaching does not give us two, three, or even four resurrections. The New Testament speaks again and again of the resurrection of just and unjust in one breath. It speaks of the Lord's coming bringing blessing to His own, and at the very same time 'destruction' to the ungodly.[1]

Note the uniform singulars: "time" not times, Daniel 12:1–2; "the hour" not hours, John 5:28–29; "day" not days, Acts 17:31; "a resurrection" not resurrections, Acts 24:15. No 1,000 years between!

Contrary to much teaching today, "the day of the Lord" is not a stretched-out period in stages covering 1,007-plus years; it is instantaneous! Wickedness and defiance ended! Judgment has come!

That Judgment is one and the same with (1) the so-called Christian judgment of works (1 Corinthians 3:15), and (2) the alleged premillennial judgment of the nations (Matthew 25:31-46).

Regarding (1) above, the Christian hope is not confidence that one will *escape* Judgment Day but confidence *for* it (see 1 John 4:17). Jesus does not teach in John 5:24 that the Christian goes unjudged. Judged, yes; condemned, no. The following Scriptures are clear. 2 Corinthians 5:10: "We must all appear before the judgment seat of Christ, that each one may be recompensed for his deeds in the body, according to what he has done, whether good or bad"; Romans 14:10, 12: ". . . we shall all stand before the judgment seat of God. . . . each of us shall give account of himself to God"; Matthew 16:27: God "will . . . recompense every man according to his deeds." When one adds to these the "every word" and "every deed" passages (Matthew 12:36; Ecclesiastes 11:9; 12:14), the most that could be hoped for on the basis of other Scriptures is that only the things confessed and forgiven will go unremembered on that one judgment day for all (Acts 17:31).

Regarding (2) above, the outcome of Matthew 25:31-46 is not a millennium but hell or heaven, and that for *all* the nations of history. This is the Judgment of Revelation 20—the Judgment before the great white throne. All *judgment* has been committed to the Son (John 5:22), though obviously the *judgment seat* of Christ and of God are the same.

Augustus Strong, one of the most eminent Baptist theologians and teachers of his day, disagreed with the two-resurrection, premillennial system which, he said, "we are combatting."[2]

> The other Scriptures contain nothing with regard to a resurrection of the righteous which is widely separated in time from that of the wicked, but rather declare distinctly that the second coming of Christ is immediately connected both with the resurrection of the just and the unjust and with the general judgment.[3]

One return. One physical resurrection. One judgment. And these three are one great climax, not requiring even twenty-four hours in execution, for then all shall know even as they are known. The saved "shall be like Him; for we shall see Him as he is" (1 John 3:2).

It is not right to teach that the Judgment need not concern the Christian because he will be elsewhere, having been judged 1,000 years earlier (and only for work rewards). No one will escape the Judgment. The teaching of Scripture on the subject of Judgment Day should awe the greatest saint.

CHAPTER 9

The Rapture and the End Are Simultaneous

Not two events but one—the saved are caught away as the world ends. This has been the understanding of the vast majority from the beginning. They find no difficulty in so believing. They have no hang-ups with prophecy; where a literal earthly interpretation would be contradictory and senseless, they understand it naturally as transcendent reality. Thus an earthly reign is out of the question. Further, both Testaments, Old and New, speak of but one climactic event, the great assize and transition, in which saved and lost participate. The flood is set forth as the example of this by Christ and by Peter.

Four principal passages now must end all doubt.

> After all it is only just for God to repay with affliction those who afflict you, and to give relief to you who are afflicted and to us as well when the Lord Jesus shall be revealed from heaven with His mighty angels in flaming fire, dealing out retribution to those who do not know God and to those who do not obey the gospel of our Lord Jesus. And these will pay the penalty of eternal destruction, away from the presence of the Lord and from the glory of His power, when He comes to be glorified in His saints on that day, and to be marveled at among all who have believed—for our testimony to you was believed (2 Thessalonians 1:6–10).

A passage such as the above could not be more plain in showing that there is but one coming or appearing or return of Christ and that this is accompanied simultaneously with the destruction and renovation of the heavens and the earth. It is evident that Paul is comforting the Thessalonians with the thought of Christ's possible coming then (with deliverance and destruction) and not 1,000 years later. But the premillennialists must interpret this passage as speaking of a later coming, for obviously if there is to be an earthly millennium, the earth cannot be destroyed at the rapture. Therefore the end of the world in this view is always no less than 1,000 years away. The passage under discussion is so plainly contrary to that idea, however, that its meaning must be twisted. It is explained that a period should be placed before the word "when," so as to allow an interpolation: "When the Lord Jesus [after the trib or mill] shall be revealed from heaven. . . ." But this changes the original meaning and intent which was to comfort the suffering Christians at Thessalonica with the hope that the Savior might come soon, bring retribution to their tormentors and relief to themselves, a double-edged event. The premillennialist interpretation of the passage is wrong grammatically. Regardless, God forbids such twisting of His words. Still, dispensationalism everywhere inserts these 1,000-year separations and pluralizings.

> *The day of the Lord* will come like a *thief,* in which the heavens will pass away with a roar and the elements will be destroyed with intense heat, and the earth and its works will be burned up. Since all these things are to be destroyed in this way, what sort of people ought you to be in holy conduct and godliness, looking for and hastening the coming of the day of God, on account of which the heavens will be destroyed by burning, and the elements will melt with intense heat! (2 Peter 3:10–12)

This is a passage that is almost untwistable. Peter's readers are admonished to be "looking for and hastening" His coming (add verses 13-14) which, clearly, will bring simultaneous destruction. To get around this, some maintain that Peter simply was not well enough informed about the day of the Lord, namely that a millennial kingdom must first run its course after Christ's coming. So the "day of the Lord" is interpreted as a stretched-out period. This does not, however, alter in the slightest the plain words of this chief apostle who had heard Christ's kingdom explanations over a period of 40 days (Acts 1:3). He too had raised the question of Acts 1:6 about the restoration of the kingdom to Israel. (Reader note: Sections of chapters 1, 10, 11 and 14 further discuss that and related questions.) Here an informed Peter says nothing about a worldly kingdom supposedly to follow Christ's return.

Now as to the times and the epochs, brethren, you have no need of anything to be written to you. For you yourselves know full well that *the day of the Lord* will come just like a *thief* in the night. While they are saying, "Peace and safety!" then destruction will come upon them suddenly like birth pangs upon a woman with child; and they shall not escape. But you, brethren, are not in darkness, that the day should overtake you like a thief (1 Thessalonians 5:1-4).

Paul's teaching here is just as clear as Peter's in showing that these Thessalonians might possibly experience the unexpected and sudden day of the Lord, which would come like a thief bringing destruction, not a mere disappearance of Christians. Paul and Peter both use the "thief" concept. This does not mean a quiet coming, but only an unexpected coming. When it comes, the heavens will pass away with a roar and the elements will be destroyed with intense heat, and the earth and its works will be burned up (2 Peter 3:10).

The end of all things is at hand; therefore, be of sound judgment and sober spirit for the purpose of prayer (1 Peter 4:7).

Here is another troublesome passage for those who hold an earthly kingdom view. Such a view certainly would contradict Peter's words, having him say, in effect, that the beginning of a Golden Age for the earth was at hand. "The end of all things" does not suggest a world intact after the rapture occurs.

Speaking of the rapture as simultaneous with the end, George Murray writes:

It has been the age-old belief of the Christian Church that God has, in His own eternal councils, appointed a day in which He shall bring the members of the human race before His judgment seat to be assigned to their eternal destinies. This belief is amply supported by the Holy Scriptures which speak of the Lord's return, the resurrection of the dead, and the final judgment, as simultaneous events. This is also suggested by the Apostles' Creed which speaks of Christ's return, and the judgment of the quick and the dead, in the same clause. In Scripture, and elsewhere, the time when this series of events shall take place is described as "the day of the Lord," or "the day of Christ."[1]

How much difference does it make, one might ask, whether a person looks for Christ's coming as the end or simply as the rapture? It makes a great deal of difference, as an Irish Presbyterian points out:

Let no one say that all this discussion matters little. The idea of the wicked being summoned to the bar of God more than a thousand years later than the righteous, tends, to say the least, to lessen 'the terror of the Lord', a terror which the Scriptures again and again seem to associate with His coming at the last trump for the great and universal assize.[2]

The same observation can be made regarding whether one looks for a secret, silent event as about to happen, or something worse than nuclear holocaust! The "tone" of one's faith is affected or, one could say, infected by the outlook. All such softening and postponing take the edge off the urgent prophecy.

There is tremendous convicting power in the proper teaching of Christ's coming as simultaneously bringing universal destruction. Spurgeon, in a sermon entitled "The World on Fire," captures the tone:

> Am I ready to be caught away to be with my Lord in the air? Or shall I be left to perish amidst the conflagration? How ought I live! How ought I to stand as it were on tip-toe, ready when He shall call me, to be away up into the glory, far off from this perishing world?[3]

Here is his invitation at the close of the sermon:

> I would to God that all here present were prepared for the future. You remember John Bunyan makes Christian sit in the City of Destruction at ease until he hears from one called Evangelist, that the city was to be burned up, and then he cries, "Alas, alas, woe is me, and I shall be destroyed in it." That thought set him running, and nothing could stop him. His wife bade him come back, but he said, "The city is to be destroyed, and I must away." His children clung about his garments to hold him, but he said "No, I must run to the City of Safety, for this city is to be burned up." Man, it will all go! If all your love is here below, it will all go! Your gold and silver will all go! Will you not have Christ? Will you not have a Savior? For if you will not, there remains for you only a fearful looking for of judgment and of fiery indignation. Tempt not the anger of God. Yield to his mercy now. Believe in His dear Son. I pray that you may this day be saved, and God be glorified in your salvation. Amen.[4]

CHAPTER 10

Israel and Israeli

"All Israel will be saved" (Romans 11:26 RSV)—"Only a remnant of them will be saved" (Romans 9:27 RSV). So a total conversion of Jewish people is not Scriptural—"all Israel" must mean something else.

There are five meanings of "Israel" in the Bible: (1) the 12 tribes; (2) the northern 10 tribes; (3) Jews (Israel according to the flesh); (4) spiritual Israel (elect Jewish believers); (5) the Israel of God (the saved, both Gentiles and Jews).

The following passages show clearly that it is a mistaken view to perpetuate the Old Testament usage of "Israel." Romans 2:28-29; 4:16-17; Galatians 3:28-29; 6:15-16; Ephesians 2:12-13; 3:6. This eliminates the first three meanings above.

Read as a unit, Romans 9-11 does not lead one to conclude that God is planning a Palestinian kingdom and a mass conversion of Jews after Christ comes. First, one should read Romans 9:1-3. These verses tell of Paul's great sorrow over the unbelief of his people according to the flesh. If it were true that conversion en masse and a glorious earthly kingdom were ahead for them, his tears were foolish. He hoped Christ might come any day! The only hope he held out for them was that the inclusion of Gentiles as the Israel of God would provoke them to repent and turn to their Messiah, as many of them have done.

Paul's inspired line of reasoning in Romans 9-11 is to praise the depth of God's riches and wisdom and knowledge, and His unfathomable ways. Nearly all Jews might have been lost, but a certain hardening in Jewry led the apostles to turn to the Gentiles (recall Acts). The inclusion of *Gentiles* as children of Abraham (Romans 9:7-8) was to make the Jews jealous (Romans 11:11, 13-14, 31), causing a remnant of them to be saved. Thus God had never rejected His people whom He foreknew (Romans 11:1, 2-5), nor has His Word failed (Romans 9:6). So in this manner *all* Israel (the true Israel of God, composed of saved Gentiles and saved Jews) will be (is being) saved. See again all Paul's Bible passages on this page. How tremendous of God!

Romans 11:26-27, citing Isaiah 59:19-21, speaks of Christ's first advent only, when the Deliverer came once for all to redeem humanity from sin. To make this yet future, and for Jews only, is falsehood.

When all the evidence is brought in, one must have the courage to say finally that even if this passage could seem to be taken either way, the one must be chosen which is in harmony with the rest of Scripture. Nothing is to be added to or taken away from Scripture in order to accommodate a scheme that allows for salvation after Christ returns.

As to the times of the Gentiles, Scripture speaks of Jerusalem as "trodden down by nations until the times of nations be fulfilled (Luke 21:24)." "Until" does not mean anything follows except Christ's coming with the end and remaking of the universe . This "fulness (Romans 11 :25)," and next the "heaven and earth shall pass away"—Luke 21:24-33 (no Jewish conversion after the "until").

The prophecy remained remarkably fulfilled despite establishment of the modern Israeli nation for a number of decades. Jerusalem continued a mixed population, with the Gentile influence remaining—an Islamic temple, the Dome of the Rock, standing on the site of the ancient Jewish temple.

That site, Mt. Zion, will not be raised physically higher than the Himalaya mountains (Mt. Everest is five and a half miles high) for a millennial reign of Christ from there. Prophecies along those lines speak simply of our greater present Gospel era in contrast to the former Old Testament era. Superior to all existing philosophies, the Gospel has been attracting all nations, as the Lord indicated, from his first advent onward, drawing all to Himself.

What will happen to the land of Palestine when the world ends? Like the rest of the world, it will be destroyed, then refashioned. Its tenants will have to move out at least temporarily. The promise that Israel was not to be dislodged again is contradictory unless applied to New Testament Israel and the heavenly inheritance (1 Chronicles 17:9-14). Israel's inheritance is the new earth (Matthew 5:5). Abraham was promised not mere Palestine but the "cosmos," according to Romans 4:13.

What significance, if any, had the reestablishment of a national Israel in 1948? Dispensationalists say it fulfilled Matthew 24:34, that the *Jewish* generation would not pass away. But every race has survived since the Flood; and the question is raised whether modern mixed "Jews" are true Jews (consult Encyclopedia Brittanica). The prophecy has been interpreted some seven other ways; which meaning is right,

God alone knows for sure. Could it be that the wrong application of this prophecy is a part of the great deception by which even the elect have been deceived?

There have been other notable returns to Palestine. Modern Israel points out that throughout the centuries Jews have returned to the land individually and in groups, and that almost every century has seen waves of immigration to the land. Edward Gibbon notes in *The History of the Decline and Fall of the Roman Empire* that such a return was granted under Julian (emperor 361-363); in it the Jews began to rebuild the temple. He speaks of respectable evidence to the effect that strange occurrences such as an earthquake, whirlwind, and a fiery eruption prevented and finally ended the effort. Some Christian writers claim that a luminous cross appeared in the heavens. A similar return had taken place about A.D. 125 under Trajan. So a checkered history has continued for that oppressed people. St. Paul points out in Romans 11:28 that as regards the election, they are beloved on account of the fathers. However, as a learned Bible teacher said, not the Jewish people, nor the Middle East, but Jesus Christ is the timepiece of prophecy.

Palestine and Israel—Christian Arabs—Christian Jews—confusing? It need not be. God loves all. He does not want His people of old or others mistreated but wants them to find true rest in this world. Yet he has a better homeland prepared for everyone who turns to Jesus the one Messiah for mankind. Above all, he wants Jew and Gentile to gain the heavenly Jerusalem.

CHAPTER 11

Which Interpretation Is Right?

The dispensational trail championed in late 20th century by Hal Lindsey's book, *The Late Great Planet Earth,* was pioneered 140 years before him. Dispensational teaching appeared in the 1830s. Its foundation is premillennialism, a most serious error that goes back to some in the early church as was seen in Chapter 4.

The Succession

EDWARD IRVING, formerly a Scottish Presbyterian minister, formed a group known as the Catholic Apostolic Church, emphasizing gifts of the Spirit in the form experienced by the early church, principally prophecy and speaking in tongues. Though he never received the gift himself, he sought a restoration of charismatic gifts, believing in a further end-time outpouring instead of understanding "the latter rain" to be the entire New Testament era ("the former rain" referring to Old Testament times). Commendably, Christ's second coming was taught with great fervor.

As has happened many times across the centuries, the church had become lethargic. At such times sincere groups arise seeking renewal. Disenchantment with the established church leads them to seek a more vital, individualistic Christian experience. Ignoring the fact that Christ promised to remain with his church though there would be weeds among the wheat, these groups forsake traditional modes in search of a direct communion, a sort of mysticism. But an observation has been made that such efforts usually begin in mist and end in schism.

Irving, via the Jesuit Lacunza's heresies, taught that Christ would return twice, not once; falsely termed stages. Defrocked for a different heresy, dying at age 42, he was buried honorably by the Church, which he had left. The stages idea may have seemed confirmed through a prophetic revelation from a young woman in Rev. Irving's church. True or not, the public account she wrote of it, reveals the revelation to be pious but incorrect. She prophesied that Christ's descent from heaven with a shout would not be something seen with "the natural eye." This of course contradicts Revelation 1:7 and six other passages which declare that *every* eye will see him at his one and only coming; these are listed on page 67. Her revelation was that only those who have "the light of God" will see his appearing and be caught up to meet him in the air. That same evening, it is recorded, she named Robert Owen, a British reformer along socialist lines, as the antichrist. He later died in the year 1858.

The "For/With" myth so much preached today began to appear in the writings of Irving. Some finalizings came later, such as never using the terms "rapture" and "appearing" interchangeably—first the secret Rapture, a coming FOR the saved; then seven years later the Appearing, a coming WITH the saved. But both simply are names for the same event! Fourteen passages prove it. In the first, Timothy is told to be faithful till the appearing. That is senseless unless rapture and appearing are the same event, else Timothy would be taken seven years before it!

-1 Timothy 6:14; 2 Timothy 4:1,8; Titus 2:13; Hebrews 9:28; 1 Peter 1:7,13; 5:4; 1 John 2:28; 3:2; Colossians 3:4; 1 Thessalonians 3:13; 4:13-18; 1 Corinthians 15:51-52. According to the latter two passages, the Lord "will bring with him" the souls, the spirits of the saved dead, to be rejoined with their resurrected, glorified bodies, as the saved living are "changed," transformed "in the twinkling of an eye:' and are "caught up together with them (the resurrected) in the clouds, to meet the Lord in the air," *instantly* joined to him, thus *appearing* also with him, Colossians 3:4! That is what the historic church has held from the beginning, even though some in these traditional groups may have forgotten or may disbelieve. By comparing the many passages listed in this paragraph, anyone can see the contradictions of the "For/With" distinction, and should agree that it is error. So is the system.

JOHN NELSON DARBY (1800-1882) was the immediate next of the succession. He knew of Irving's work, visited the revival scene, but seems not to have approved of it. He too was critical of the church. Born in London, he had attended law college in Dublin, and became an Anglican Priest in Ireland. Later he made frequent trips to America where he travelled and taught extensively. He is considered to be "the father of dispensationalism."

Considering the church a lost cause due to formalism and spiritual barrenness, he encouraged pastors and parishioners to leave it. He led a movement aimed at establishing a pure church. Soon it split into several groups known as "Plymouth Brethren" or simply "Brethren." To allow the Holy Spirit free sway, they used no set order in worship.

Though there is no evidence of it in his writings, as a researcher points out, Darby thought years later he had become convinced of the secret rapture about 1827—that would place it before the "revelation" (see on page 76) at Irving's church; however, there had been much afoot in revival circles about the doctrine of the second advent for the idea to have begun in him, and to seem validated by others open to making Biblical distinctions not previously taught by the historic church. The young woman may have been primed by those goings on.

The distinction already was present in premillennialism, only that the rapture, its "first resurrection," was followed afterwards by the appearing and return to reign. Darby simply added the unscriptural ideas of a "secret" rapture followed by a "parenthesis" or seven-year postponement, which opened the door to filling the gap with Daniel's 70th 7 (supposedly Revelation 4-19). Such wild dividing of Scripture could make out a case for almost anything, someone has pointed out.

B. W. Newton, at first an associate of Darby, became a defector. Of the secret rapture, he declared that the whole testimony of Scripture was against it. And when Darby's parenthesis doctrine began to be taught, Newton said that the secret rapture was bad enough, but that this was worse. Read Sandeen for further details on this succession.

W. E. BLACKSTONE, a Methodist minister, became a dispensationalist and later left his denomination. He too was turned off and spoke of "the apostate church." He wrote the most influential book in support of the premillennial-dispensational-pretributational position, titled *Jesus Is Coming*. Even though the Lindsey book has outsold it, the Blackstone book convinced many pastors as well as laity. It was not only popularly sold but effectively distributed gratis by generous funding and planned efforts. Published in 1898, a 1932 edition on the title page stated it had been issued in forty languages and no less than 1,000,330 copies by that date. It is still selling.

According to Sandeen, a republication of it was provided by two wealthy Stewart brothers. In 1908 they had a list made of English speaking missionaries, theological students and professors, and paid for free distribution to them of Blackstone's book.

Another generous outreach later, if the account is accurate, was undertaken by a Bible institute. The writer was sent this information in 1978 by an elderly Assembly of God gentleman, who in commenting that there should be a Full Gospel Amillennial Denomination, stated in his letter, "It was a shame that the Assemblies were caught up in that heresy in early days," adding, "The Assemblies have always been right in every doctrine except eschatology. I suppose you know that the 'Prophecy' Conferences in the 1880s and 1890s were the main cause of the church as a whole accepting Premillennialism"—whether he meant all churches or only his own group cannot be said, for contact with him was lost some ten years later—the letter goes on, "and also that the Moody outfit in Chicago sent to nearly every Protestant Pastor the Blackstone book in about 1910 or round about."

To show the profound effect that mistaken millennialism produces, he went on to say, "Back in the early part of the 20th century the Pentecostal preachers would preach mostly Judgment Day and the burning of earth and Jesus second coming, and got the name of 'doomsday preachers'; then after the Scofield 1917 Bible, it changed them."

Blackstone seems to have forgotten balanced theology, adopting instead a selective literalism with proof texts. Literal only where it suits, is how one has characterized such handling of the Bible. One of the most misleading things in his book is the mixing of Bible clauses taken out of context and inserted into other verses. This criticism obviously had been voiced by others in prior encounters with Blackstone, for on page 163 he stated, "It is objected that we have no right thus to bring together these passages from different parts of the Word. We answer— why not? Are they not all inspired? Are they not all the product of one mind?" What Herbert T. Meyer calls reducing Scripture to a "wax nose" could well apply to such mixing.

CYRUS I. SCOFIELD was a convinced premillennial dispensation-alist Christian before he produced the Bible that bears his name. A biased approach to the Bible is the most dangerous hermeneutic (man-ner of interpreting). For the question applies, On what do you bias your opinion? Many of his references, notes and headings are acceptable and helpful. But that is error's way, which few people understand. Error comes in the guise of light via many who are sincere but wrong. The Scofield Reference Bible is just this: the Bible interpreted by premillen-nial presuppositions with the further errors of dispensationalism.

Unfortunately most do not know well the whole of Scripture or are not analytically minded. New converts and the young receive unsound teaching with childlike acceptance, including distrust of the ancient church. They become like pre-exposed film. Someone has said that it takes three to six months to become skilled in the premillennial dispen-sational system by the promptings of the Scofield Bible. But truth is stronger than error. Before departing this life, Dr. Harry Rimmer wrote: "For twenty years I also believed and taught that the Roman Empire would be restored . . . I did not realize that I was teaching interpretation of the text in place of the Word itself." Seeing what is not there, and blindness to the natural meaning or understanding, are the result of sys-tem interpretation.

By now in this book the basic tenets of the Scofield Bible, 1909, have been made known. In our concluding chapter on safeguards, more will be said concerning its influence and concerning other matters relat-ed to that system as well as alternate views. But here in this chapter, sev-eral clarifications of the fold-out chart (page 54) will be made.

Talk of the End as only the end of an age, as in his Bible notes, has grown; it was predictable that its literalization of Palestine forever would lead to denial of an utterly destroyed present earth and heavens, from which arise the promised new earth and new heavens. Its detouring dou-ble talk ignores that 1) no further age ever is mentioned as coming after the End except heaven, and 2) Palestine forever is a bold denial of all the Bible which teaches clearly a re-make of puny Palestine and all into greater country, Paradise. How serious to abrogate our Lord's dictum, "The heaven and the earth shall pass away" (Matthew 24:35), and as stated by His chief disciple, "But the day of the Lord shall come as a thief in night, in which the heavens shall pass away with rushing roar, and the elements burning with heat shall be demolished, and earth and the works in it shall be *consumed* with fire" (2 Peter 3:10). It is common now to hear hints if not outright teaching that the burning of earth will be "surface only." In other works, Dr. Scofield has said: "There was NO END after all, but continuity, change, development–a new heaven and a new earth." No! A fallen ruined world *cremated*, said one; a temporal universe destroyed to become an eternal one, pledges the Creator.

Resurrecting resurrections is a dispie skill. It equates the ongoing spiritual hour of John 5:25 with 5:28, making it a 1,007 year *physical* resurrection hour! thus inventing four: (a) the Rapture phase at Revelation 4:1; (b) an Appearing phase at Luke 14:14. See fold out chart, page 54. Making Luke 14:14's "resurrection of the just" a separate one (needed in its system) could be called silly were it not so serious. The just will reap what they have sown, as will the unjust, on the day of resurrection (Acts 24:15 and all the Bible). You, dear reader, share in Luke 14: 14 along with "just Lot" (2 Peter 2:7) and every person made just through Christ since Adam and Eve ("the spirits of the just who have been perfected," Hebrews 12:23) if you have the same hope. Twice more, dispieism needs resurrection or rapture: (c) for the saved dead during its millennium, and saved living at its end; (d) of all history's wicked at their millennium's end. But read Jesus, John 5:28-29; 6:39-44; 11:24. So, there is *one* last day! with *one* physical resurrection!

HAL LINDSEY, a graduate of the dispensational School of Theology, Dallas Theological Seminary, authored *The Late Great Planet Earth* in 1970. It went through twenty-six printings in the first year and a half, with 1,700,000 copies in print already then.

His system is the same as the rest but with more identifications. His final generation (not 25 but 40 years) dated from the 1948 "restoration" of Israelis. Thus, his Rapture year was to be by 1988 "or so." Instead, the Bible locates the Jewish restoration in 538 B.C. (Edict of Cyrus) and in the present Gospel era (the saved remnant).

> People whose hopes are often incited to expect the fulfillment of what they accept as prophecy are equally disappointed when their hopes do not materialize. The result is that some lose faith in the Scriptures, rather than in those who undertake to interpret them.[1]

He speculates that nations not named in the Bible nevertheless may be identified such as the now European Union, America, China, Russia, unaware that Satan deceives by false systems and events of the day.

> The New Testament simply does not contain any predictions which apply to certain specific present-day nations or states, to these and to these only. It describes the struggle between the church and the world. It says nothing that refers exclusively or even specifically to China, Japan, the Netherlands, or Louisiana![2]

Satan is a sower, a grower, a builder. The big "clue" of the restoration of Israel in unbelief, whether 538 B.C. or conjectured as A.D. 1948, was no prediction. Jewish unbelief was the lament of the prophets of old; Israel's restoration in 538 B.C. was prophesied and fulfilled, as well as the remnant's "return to God" with Gentiles to the end of time, being grafted in again throughout Christian history. As for non-Bible dispie prophecies of a modern restoration of the twelve tribes of Israel, such "light" did not come from above. Further, as Dr. Lowry's writings point out, there are no tribes to restore.

Brother Lindsey's literalism compared to the literalism of the historic faith doesn't compare. The historic faith believes "stars" (Revelation 6) to be stars, as Jesus says also in Matthew 24, "the stars will fall from heaven." Lindsey interprets these "stars" to be Russian missiles. Enough said.

Lindsey and the others teach that Christ will intervene to save us from self-destruction. The historic faith totally disagrees as follows: CHRIST is the hope of the world, NOT Christ's coming; Christ's coming is the DOOM of the unsaved world!

Horrible Heresies. In this writer's opinion, that false hope held out to the world ranks third in the worst heresies of all time, which in order are: 1) an end to hell; 2) universal salvation; 3) being saved after Christ comes; 4) Christ can't come yet. The most harmful teaching of Lindsey is that, after Christ comes, 144,000 Jewish Billy Graham's will win the greatest number of converts in all history! A person who teaches that system may be a Christian soul-winner, but what a champion for the truth he might have been.

CHAPTER 12

The Handwriting of the Heavens

It is a great spiritual tragedy of our times, this writer feels, that a large segment of the evangelical church has been taught to understand the Bible premillennially and postmillennially. This is tragic for a number of reasons, not least of which is the failure to use the impact of the space age to advantage.

An explanation is in order. It is this: unless the End is looked for (not prior events, nor a millennium first, nor a secret coming of Christ with a millennium following seven years later) one will not rightly feel the full impact of the nuclear age. The outlook is blunted. Moreover, in such a case, that note not only is diminished in one's own perception, but he fails to project it in his witness.

The language of our Lord was unmistakable. He spoke of the end of the world, never of a secret rapture. This approach by the Son of God is well calculated and should be much employed in the present hour. But that impact is blunted in the thinking and tone of those who do not look for the end as at hand since it is always, in their view, at least 1,000 years away, as stated in chapter 9.

Astronomy is this writer's hobby. One vivid impression it makes is that the massive destruction of the heavens and earth spoken of in the Bible is happening constantly on a smaller scale throughout the universe as a star here or there becomes a super nova, i.e., explodes, disintegrating areas as vast as the solar system of our star, the sun. *No star is forever*—dying by an explosion process or as a result of entropy, i.e. heat dissipation, by which the universe is wearing out like a garment (Isaiah 51:6), but is to be ended by God (2 Peter 3). Science says: "The universe as we know it was born, and it will die."

Our present knowledge of the universe and a right understanding of Biblical teaching have moved closer, not farther apart. The Bible never taught that the earth is flat or that the universe is three-storied. From its holy and revealing pages men might have guessed that the earth is not stationary but in motion and that the universe is composed of orbiting bodies. The Word of God is always more up-to-date than scientific knowledge which at best trails far behind. Further disclosures of God's creative witness may be expected as time and discovery continue, God granting.

Some utterances of God's Word have become intelligible only in our time, such as: the circle of the earth (Isaiah 40:22), earth reeling to and fro like a drunkard (Isaiah 24:20), courses (Judges 5:20), risings and circuits (Psalm 19:6). Job 26:7 states, "He . . . hangs the earth on nothing." Teachings such as eternity itself, the bottomless pit, perpetual fire, end of the world physically—these make sense. Thus the teaching of everlasting hellfire means that very thing, not just a burning conscience that people fearlessly have even now.

Creation's witness in this space age is greater than ever. Psalm 19:1 says it pointedly to this century and any yet to come:

The heavens are telling of the glory of God;
And their expanse is declaring the work of His hands.

Here inspired David thinks of all God's vast creation, particularly of the heavenly bodies—the stars, our sun and moon, and of the firmament or atmosphere that surrounds us.

In other psalms, simply, yet majestically, he sings the praises of our great Creator as he regards the wonders of the earth and the marvel that he is "fearfully and wonderfully made" (Psalm 139:14).

Truly nature is one vast, effective sermon; and never more so than in a scientific age. Someone has referred to sun, moon, and stars as God's "traveling preachers." Joseph Addison put it:

The spacious firmament on high,
With all the blue ethereal sky,
And spangled heavens, a shining frame,
Their great Original proclaim.
The unwearied sun from day to day
Does his Creator's power display,
And publishes to every land
The works of an almighty hand.

Soon as the evening shades prevail
The moon takes up the wondrous tale,
And nightly to the listening earth
Repeats the story of her birth;
Whilst all the stars that round her burn,
And all the planets in their turn,

Confirm the tidings as they roll,
And spread the truth from pole to pole.

What though in solemn silence all
Move round the dark terrestrial ball;
What though no real voice nor sound
Amid their radiant orbs be found;
In reason's ear they all rejoice,
And utter forth a glorious voice,
Forever singing as they shine,
"The hand that made us is divine."

The heavens declare not only the existence of God but also His *glory*. How do they do this? By showing order, power, beauty; by hinting of eternity; by displaying God's patience, faithfulness, mercy, love, destructive power; His wisdom, His inexhaustibleness—the list grows long.

The witness of nature is powerful. "Declare" and "proclaim" are forceful words. The manifold works of nature point to God as their source. In wisdom He made them all. His painstaking care is seen in everything. Deposited on the moon by our astronauts, are these words:

O Lord, our Lord
  How majestic is Thy name in all the earth,
  Who hast displayed Thy splendor above the heavens!
  From the mouth of infants and nursing babes
    Thou hast established strength,
  Because of Thine adversaries,
  To make the enemy and the revengeful cease.

When I consider Thy heavens, the work of Thy fingers,
  The moon and the stars, which Thou hast ordained;
  What is man, that Thou dost take thought of him?
  And the son of man, that Thou dost care for him?
  Yet Thou hast made him a little lower than God,
  And dost crown him with glory and majesty! (Psalm 8:1–5)

Much still remains unknown. It is a deception to think that a full disclosure of all the truth waits just around the corner. The years ahead will bring greater witness to the truth of God's Word as well as denials more bold and blind than ever. Someone has asked:

I have a life in Christ to live;
I have a death in Christ to die;
And must I wait till science give
All doubts a full reply?

It should be remembered that God will not judge us on the basis of what science says for or against Him, but on what *He* says.

There never was, nor is there today, any real excuse for unbelief. The Bible states, "Ever since the creation of the world His invisible nature, namely, his eternal power and deity, has been clearly perceived in the things that have been made. So they are without excuse" (Romans 1:20 RSV). It is neither intelligent nor reasonable to deny God's existence. "The fool has said in his heart, 'There is no God' " (Psalm 14:1). Matter eternal instead of a Creator? Insanity!

In the first words of the Bible, God gives us our bearings—"In the beginning God created the heavens and the earth" (Genesis 1:1). Without this declaration and explanation, we would be living in a baffling, meaningless, purposeless universe. And this creating was EX NIHILO, out of nothing; for our minds tell us that before time there was eternity, before matter there was empty space—not a particle of dust, not a wisp of air, not an atom, no components of any kind, known or unknown. Matter and radiation, called "the two constituents of the physical universe," did not then exist and could not have come into existence except by miracle. Albert Einstein too said that of course "a Divine fiat" (act of creation) was demanded. Psalm 33:9, "He spoke, and it came to be; he commanded, and it stood forth." Hebrews 11:3 affirms ex nihilo.

Until original creation is acknowledged, any talk of evolution is unfounded, illogical, as empty as once was space the four to many billion years ago when the present universe was born, according to calculations of science. So our very existence is standing proof of the Eternal Omnipotent God who made us and all that exists, visible and invisible. And in the moment that the Lord comes, all, living and dead, shall know the truth which cried out from everything—His creative power and genius and providence. Someone expresses it: the mountains—God's majestic thoughts; the stars—God's brilliant thoughts; the flowers—God's beautiful thoughts.

Evidences include vastness, an infinite God. Signs in the heavens (including exceptions which disprove mechanism) point to an end, even as earthly evidence confirms a destructive flood. 70% of the earth remains covered by water. 2 Peter 3:3-7 is so relevant at this point, reader, that you are asked to consult it. (Pause)

Therefore Christians living in the space age must be decided and fervent witnesses, and should be knowledgeable. But wonderful as it is to know that God the Son is "upholding the universe by His word of power" (Hebrews 1:3 RSV), it is more wonderful still to know Him as Savior. A story is told of an atheist in London who tried to embarrass an uneducated man who had been converted. "Do you know anything about Christ?" he asked. "Yes, by the grace of God, I do," was the answer. "When was He born?" The ignorant saint gave an incorrect answer. "How old was He when He died?" Again the answer was incorrect. The atheist said with a sneer, "See, you do not know so much about Jesus after all, do you?" "I know all too little," was the modest reply, "but I know this: I was one of the worst drunkards in London. My wife was a brokenhearted woman; my children were afraid of me. Today I have one of the happiest homes in London. Jesus has done this for me. This I know."

The Christian heritage in this space age is awesome. It is to be a pressing reminder that "unto whomsoever much is given, of him shall be much required" (Luke 12:48 KJV).

Greater light—greater responsibility! The persuaded of planet earth must endeavor in love by life and word to persuade other earth dwellers.

In a day of much denial there is need for renewed affirmation. Not only must one insist on the virgin birth and physical resurrection of Christ, but also on His bodily return and the physical end of the world—the literal transformation to the new heavens and new earth. Those who treat the very end of the world figuratively must reckon with our Lord's pledge that the heavens will suffer the end as well (Matthew 24:35). Christ teaches that the end is being physically forecast by signs in sun and moon and stars, by world-wide earthquakes (studies show increasing frequency and possibly magnitude) and famine, by sea and waves roaring, and by the signs of the times themselves.

Our churches should be overflowing, "all the more, as you see the day drawing near" (Hebrews 10:25).

CHAPTER 13

The Unknowable in Things to Come

A Jesuit pointed out that there have always been two errors regarding the Lord's return: having Him come too soon or too far away.

There is a paradox in Scripture regarding the unknowable extent of Christ's kingdom. On the one hand, Christ could have come at any time; on the other, it is indicated that the extent of the kingdom is unlimited.

The glorious expectation held out in such passages as Isaiah 2, with all nations streaming to the Lord, and knowledge of the Lord covering the earth, with all knowing Him, from the least to the greatest, must be balanced with more sobering statements. The Lord spoke of the wide gate, at which many go in to destruction, and the narrow way to life, which few find. The disciples knew what He had said about going into all the world and about His possible or seeming delay in returning. They had learned the parables on readiness and hintings of delay. They went forth with the message, not knowing how many they could reach until He returned. They certainly did not think that He could not return until they reached everyone. Peter, John, Jude, and James, the Lord's brother, not to mention Paul and the writer of Hebrews, whether Paul or another, *all* expected the Lord's return. This is very significant. They knew His teaching better than we. They knew the Old Testament and how the great covenant blessings were to be understood. Peter was sharp on these matters. He saw by inspiration that Christ was on David's throne by virtue of the resurrection (Acts 2:30–31). He knew the extent of the Abrahamic covenant. Yet he looked for Christ's return as a very real possibility in his day—in terms of destruction and refashioning.

Neither the parables hinting of Christ's possible delay nor any suggesting possibly a greater extent of outreach kept them from looking for His return in their lifetime. Peter looked for it—2 Peter 3 and 1 Peter 4:7. John looked for it—1 John 2:18, 28 and 3:2, not to mention references throughout the Book of Revelation. Jude looked for it—Jude 17–18, 21. James, the Lord's brother, looked for it—James 5:7-9. Paul looked for it—1 Cor. 15:51–57; Philippians 4:5; 1 Thessalonians 3:13;

4:13-18; 5:1-4; 2 Thessalonians 1:6-10; 2 Timothy 4:1; Titus 2:13. Hebrews sees "the day drawing near (10:25)."

The chief problem perhaps is the statement of Matthew 24:14: "This Gospel of the kingdom shall be preached in the whole world for a witness to all the nations, and then the end shall come."

> This does not mean that every individual must hear, much less be saved. It means the nations as a whole will have opportunity given to them and that there will be those out of every nation among the redeemed (Rev. 7:9).[1]

It is a greater error than dispensationalism if we press this worldwide extent meaning too far. Archbishop Richard Trench most wisely said, "The Second Advent is possible any day, impossible no day."

In Romans 16:26, the apostle Paul states that the Gospel of Jesus Christ "has been made known to all nations" and in Colossians 1:23, he speaks of the Gospel as having been "proclaimed in all creation under heaven." And they hoped to see His return.

The following is an interesting commentary on this question of the extent of Christ's Kingdom.

> The question is often asked—Will the world become better or worse towards the coming of the Lord? There are passages in the Bible which seem to teach very clearly that the world at His coming will be a very wicked place like the world of Noah's Day or of Lot's day (e.g., Matt. 24:37-42). And there are other passages which seem to set forth a gradual development of Christ's kingdom (e.g., Matt. 13:31-33). Both pictures are, no doubt, true. As R. B. Kuiper says: "Broadly speaking, conditions on earth are becoming better and worse at once. Witness the Christianization of pagan nations and the slipping back of Christian people into paganism." It is likely that "as the reign of the truth will be gradually extended, so the power of evil will gather force towards the end."[2]

CHAPTER 14

Safeguards for Things to Come

It is bad to teach that He must come now.

It is worse to teach that He cannot come yet.

It is worst of all to teach that He will not be coming back.

The following facts should keep one safe from the first danger named above (dispensationalism):

1) No salvation after Christ's return
2) The rapture and the end are simultaneous
3) The binding of Satan is not future
4) Christ is reigning now
5) An earthly millennium contradicts Christ, creeds, and all the Bible
6) Supposedly millennial Old Testament passages speak of "forever" conditions
7) Old Testament Israel has been replaced

As for teaching that He cannot come yet (postmillennialism), the Savior's own words are the best safeguard. (More at page 92.)

As for any who think He will not be back, because they think there will be no end, let it be remembered that we live in a real universe which had a real and momentary beginning. Is it not reasonable also from a scientific standpoint to reckon with the real possibility that it will end in the same manner? Then too, for those who turn the whole Bible into one vast allegory, it should be borne in mind that symbols in the Bible mean more than they say, not less.

George Murray said it well: "We take second place to no one in our conviction that the Lord will return personally and visibly."[1]

With prophecy it should be borne in mind that spiritual realities may have earthly accompaniments. It may well be, for example, that the beasts of Revelation 13 will find their ultimate, deepest, and final fulfillment in a coalition of political and an apostatized church, by and large. However, it is doubtful that Armageddon is both a spiritual and physical war of global dimensions at the last, triggered in the Middle

East. The prophecy is spiritual. Even darkest times may not yet exhaust God's longsuffering. Further deliverance may come and the final advent of Christ not yet arrive. See Genesis 18:22-32, and 2 Chronicles 7:14.

Signs are indeed all around us. There *is* some significance to today's headlines. Our salvation is nearer every day, as the Word of God points out. There is an intensifying and deepening; and of course one generation *will* be the last.

Meanwhile it is wise that no one be wise in his own conceits. It should not be surprising to find true believers at opposite poles in matters of end-time prophecy. Recall Calvinism and Arminianism, both systems based on Scripture. This is not to say that nothing is conclusive, but it should provide an escape valve for those locked into schools of interpretation which prove to be erroneous. Sign-seeking and piecemeal views are dangers, but equally so is insensitivity to proper Scriptural signs of the times–general but ever closer!

There is no way to reconcile differences between postmillennialism and premillennialism and amillennialism. There is no way to ignore such serious matters which affect all aspects of the faith. Speaking the truth in love (Ephesians 4:15) does not cancel speaking it. Love for truth demands debate in the Word, as in this book. The Christian community should be made aware, at least, that there are alternative viewpoints held by Bible believers who look for the transition of the heavens and earth and to enjoyment of God's kingdom forevermore.

The argument really is not between the literal and the spiritual, but between the earthly and the transcendent, both of which are literal. It is well to remember, as stated before, that earthly symbols do not mean less but more. That principle guards against either restricting the meaning of figurative language or robbing it of reality.

The writer is willing to furnish samples and suggestions for conducting seminars on "Things to Come and Not to Come." He invites the reader to make inquiry, urging that true prophetic interpretation be sought diligently in this time of stress. That this is essential is demonstrated in something Corrie ten Boom once said. She has been referred to as a great-aunt to all the saints, having herself graced a Nazi prison camp, and to the Orient and Europe—on both sides of the Iron Curtain. She has been quoted in many sources as follows:

> There are some among us teaching there will be no tribulation, that the Christians will be able to escape all this. These are the false teachers Jesus was warning us to expect in the latter days. Most of them have little knowledge of what is already going on across the world.

I have been in countries where the saints are already suffering terrible persecution. In China the Christians were told, "Don't worry, before the tribulation comes, you will be translated—raptured." Then came a terrible persecution. Millions of Christians were tortured to death. Later I heard a Bishop from China say, sadly, "We have failed. We should have made the people strong for persecution rather than telling them Jesus would come first."

Turning to me he said, "You still have time. Tell the people how to be strong in times of persecution, how to stand when the tribulation comes—to stand and not faint."

What if the midnight knock comes before the midnight shout? That is to say, what if the secret police come before the Bridegroom comes? Dare anyone be absolutely certain it will not be, and teach people so? Things *are* coming for planet earth. Each needs to know these matters rightly. The best assurance to be found is that *He is* coming. Each must face the very personal questions: Am I ready? Am I correctly and sufficiently informed? Am I equipped for any eventuality?

Where do we go from here? Up, of course, whether we live or die. Thanks be to God! It is the Christian's constant encouragement that "the coming of the Lord is at hand" (James 5:8).

Trib Trap

Note in the above quotation that "tribulation" is understood to be an identifiable period yet future—"before the tribulation comes." This is a trap because, while what we have said on page 40 is true, it is true also that tribulation is not a *discernible* period, nor necessarily worldwide. "There shall be then great tribulation such as has not been from the beginning of the world until now, no, nor ever shall be" (Matthew 24:21)—"These are they who come out of the great tribulation, and they washed their robes, and made their robes white in the blood of the Lamb" (Revelation 7:14); but those passages must be understood as unknowable as to the when or how long, even for Christians; for to the time of the physical End, at least much of the world will be absorbed in business as usual. "For as the days of Noah," Jesus says, "so shall be also the coming of the Son of man.... before the flood, eating and drinking, marrying and giving in marriage, until the day Noah entered into the ark, and they knew not till the flood came and swept them all away" (Matthew 24:37-39)—"For when they may say, Peace and security, then sudden destruction comes upon them" (1 Thessalonians 5:3). No further tribulation, nothing need happen, before the world can end.

91

Great debate goes on between pre- post- and mid-tribulation rapturists—whether the Rapture is to come before, after, or during their "great tribulation." Insofar as they mean a future 7-year tribulation, all three are in error. The pre-tribbies (most every dispensationalist) have a great advantage, because everyone would like to believe that way, so as to escape suffering. (This kind of talk is a stumbling-block, as shall be seen in our next section.) Also, the flesh inclines to postmillennialism and premillennialism, even as the flesh inclines to pretribulationism. Apologies for this complicated language, but it is not the fault of the simple historic faith.

God alone knows the whens and how longs of everything. At all times there is plenty of tribulation in the world, especially for Christians, making it impossible to say that "the tribulation" has not come. Remember, "It is not for you to know times or seasons," Christ says in Acts 1:7.

Christ-Can't-Come-Yet Folly

It is incredible that any should hold the above. Even though in sketching things to come, Jesus told the disciples "But the end is not yet" (Matthew 24:6), they are included as possible End-participants throughout the discourse. It is clear from His words and from their writings as shown in our preceding chapter, that they also were to be ready for His possible second coming in their lifetimes. So the "not yet" limitation ran out in that first century. To use "the end is not yet" to support postmillennial teaching still thousands of years later is, to say the least, foolish.

Using other bits of Scripture that may seem to overrule the Christ of Scripture is strange debate. Yet postmills and post-tribs use such to argue against His "any-moment coming" teaching. It is such weak soup, but for a complete menu one must give a bit of space to those so-called "intervening events" and "non-imminent" arguments. They are: 1) the 2 Thessalonians 2 "falling away first"; 2) Peter and Paul's expectation of death by martyrdom rather than Christ's coming; 3) John's possibly continuing longer than the others (John 21:22). Other tidbits are weaker still and need not take space.

As for 1) in the foregoing paragraph, apostasy always is present sufficiently, and the revealing of antichrist may be momentary in connection with Christ's coming, so as to render the argument void. Arguments 2) and 3) do not rule out that, though they knew their deaths were at hand, John's later, yet Christ might still have come, for He had said that only the Father knew that "when." Further, in Peter's case, the argument is based on 2 Peter 1:14 (Paul's on 2 Timothy 4:6), but it overlooks his statement two chapters later, "Nevertheless *we,* according to his promise, look for new heavens and a new earth" (2 Peter 3:13)—bearing in mind that this meant looking for Christ's coming and Peter's possibly seeing it, he could not know which might come first, his death or Christ's arrival with the End.

The writer sincerely prays that the overly optimistic hopes of post-millennialism plus the "trib trap" and "not yet" stumbling-blocks are now removed, and that the reader believes Christ's coming could occur at this very reading moment.

Chart Clarifications

"Revelation 20 only" in the historic faith (fold-out chart, page 54) means that only what is said *there* applies. Figurative Old Testament prophecies are not transported into Revelation 20. Their interpretation by Christ's New Testament forbids a literal dominion over the world by the Church or by a restored Israel, and also forbidden is a special time of millennial prosperity or flourishing; rather, a spreading of Gospel blessings through the Church to all the world, and blessings in heaven, were the glorious meaning intended by Old Testament prophecies.

Antichrist, as understood by the historic faith from the Roman Emperors onward, is seen within history up to Christ's coming. Amillennial opinion favors a line or collective personification, rather than a one and only person. It is of note, as Boettner points out, that the King James and American Standard versions did not capitalize the term, indicating that the translators saw antichrist as not one particular individual. Personifications are common in the Bible, of course—"Blessed is the *man*" (whoever and all), Psalm 1; "God is in the midst of *her* (the city of God)," Psalm 46; "the *bride* of Christ"; and so on. The New King James Version capitalizes the term in 1 John 2:18 and 4:3, telling something of its translators.

The rest of the fold-out chart is explained throughout this book.

Current Concerns

NOT FROM GOD. The diverse and strange teachings examined in this book are not due to differences in the Bible, but to differences of human interpretation. Many say the differences came through Bible study, but some admit that their system's light is not found in the teachings of Jesus but came rather from the Holy Spirit who was to reveal things to come. Jesus did say of the Holy Spirit (John 16:13) that He would show the apostles things to come (the original Greek for "show" can indicate repetition, "show *again*"), but that "He will not speak from himself." In the next verses (14-15) our Lord twice states that this showing or teaching of the Holy Spirit would not be the Holy Spirit's own, but "out of mine He will receive (take, get)." In that same evening's discourses with, note, only the apostles, Christ assured them that the Holy Spirit would teach and bring to their remembrance all things which He (Jesus) had said to them. Even if the Lord had revealed new truth to the Holy Spirit, such truth would be contained in the apostles' writings, which, apart from systems, is not there.

THIEF IN THE DAY. Adding to God's Word will add the damning plagues of the Book of Revelation (22:18); taking away from God's Word will result in God's taking away one's part in the Book of Life (22:19). To illustrate this grave importance, think of a business firm with a branch overseas. It cables the home office as to whether a vast amount should be loaned a party. Immediately the home office cables back: "Not good for any amount." But someone transmitting the cable adds an "e" to Not. That meant ruin. Or turn the story around— "Note" was meant, but the "e" was left off. The applicant is ruined. Of infinitely greater, eternal importance is the right transmission of God's truth.

It is most dangerous to say that Christ's teachings really are not for us except in some limited ways. Philip Mauro a dispensationalist formerly, using the Sermon on the Mount (Matthew 5-7) as one example, later charged that dispensationalism "classes these sayings of our Lord with the law of Sinai, and relegates them to a Jewish kingdom somewhere in the future" *(The Gospel of the Kingdom,* page 162). Speaking of the tender affection for the four accounts of the Gospel which the Lord's people have had throughout the Christian era, but which are being applied to a supposed future generation of "Israel after the flesh," he related how the very day after writing that paragraph came a letter from a missionary in Africa in which he stated his conviction that a great many of the Lord's people "are suffering from a lack of application of the truths of our Lord's Ministry, *in the Gospels,* to their daily lives." "Grace—in Epistles, not Gospels," Scofield page 989!

This is truly thievery in broad daylight! At the same time, the Law is maligned instead of being honored as "holy, just, and good," Romans 7:12. Mauro said that dispensationalism instills in the people of God an aversion toward His law; and the impression is given that to be "under the law" is the next thing to being in the lake of fire. These two sample dispensationalizing extremes of putting Christ on legal ground and of downgrading the law must be avoided. Most do, no doubt, but users of the Scofield Reference Bible must use caution—do read John 1:17.

So must we all. *A telegram to Christians of all stripes:* Let Christ the Word have the supreme place within and over all the Bible! "Hear Him!", Moses and Elijah are told on the Mount of Transfiguration. "The words that I speak to you are spirit and are life" (John 6:63); He does not say "spirit and life as are all other Scriptures," but that His, the words of the Word, are unique, decisive, over all, the plumb line. "In many parts and in many ways of old God having spoken to the fathers in the prophets, in these last days spoke to us in Son" (so reads the original). He is all, and subject to no dispensations!

THE LETTER KILLETH. It is Christ who decides whether a thing is to be understood literally or figuratively. How sad, how tragic, that in the name of literalism the Bible has been 'wrongly divided,' chopped to bits.

One can turn into stone what God intended for bread. Jewish interpretation does that, making no distinction between spiritual and temporal; it sees the scenery but misses the play. So also, post- and premillennialism let the Old Testament override the New, contrary to the age-old dictum of the historic faith—"the New is in the Old concealed, the Old is in the New revealed." Another: His testimony, ours; His silence, ours.

Oh what a shame that stalwart evangelicals should make shipwreck on the shores of literalism. Instead of following Christ's lead in the transition of covenants, phasing out the Old and phasing in the New harmoniously, dispensational futurism retains the Old and New in conflict, doublings, confusion, gaps, insertions, distinctions, discriminations, and in such contradictory complexity that the average Christian or pastor cannot disentangle it but simply accepts it as higher knowledge by the greats.

One can literalize away the spiritual as well as spiritualize away the literal. To Christ's question, "What do you think of the Christ? Whose son is he?" the literal answer by the Pharisees was only, "The son of David" (Matthew 22:42), missing the greater meaning.

Post- pre- and dispie systems are not consistently literal as to Christ's teachings. Let us paraphrase Him:

—"With your world conversion ideas, you do not take literally my words, 'Many are called but few are chosen' or 'the way that leads to life is narrow, and few there be that find it' ";

95

—"Literally my kingdom is not, and never will be, of a worldly nature as you make it";

—"Literally, the kingdom comes not with outward observation, such as the latest Jewish return to Palestine which started in 1948, which you mistakenly interpret—beware of 'Lo here! lo there' as I fore-warned";

—"Literally there shall be one fold, not two as you teach; one shepherd, not I with the 'bride' (Gentiles) and my Father with the 'wife' (Jewish)—you are quite wrong in such distinctions";

—"If you will receive it, John the Baptizer literally fulfilled the prophecy that Elijah must first come—he *has* come—Elijah will not be reincarnated";

—"The kingdom literally is in you and among you—how do you read Colossians 1:13?—it will never be a kingdom with literal Jerusalem headquarters, for I need no earthly throne, and will not sit on one, thank you all the same—truly, truly, I say to you, my kingdom is now and forever, and I am reigning now and forever, literally";

—"I have many things to say to you literally, but you cannot bear them now."

Post- pre- and dispie systems are not consistently literal as to the rest of the Bible either. Again let us paraphrase:

—"Forever means literally forever, not 1,000 years";

—" '. . . that the Gentiles are fellow heirs, of the same body (Ephesians 3:6),' you do not take literally in keeping two bodies";

—"The favorable prophecies of Moses about the future of Israelites you see, and likewise the favorable part of Daniel's 70 7s, but in both you fail to take literally the forecasts of the end of the Old Covenant in desolations until the consummation (End of all things)";

—"Believers literally '*have* come to Mount Zion and to the city of the living God, the heavenly Jerusalem (Hebrews 12:22)'—fulfillment does not await a physical, worldly Mount Zion and Jerusalem, nor a conversion period during a future trib or a 1,000 year millennium";

—"Literally the whole world will end; Palestine is not forever";

—"Jerusalem that is above and comes down from above, replaces Jerusalem below, literally";

—"The heavenly promises to Abraham and David cannot be fulfilled literally in worldly confines";

—"Literally not all Jews will be saved, but only a remnant of both Jews and Gentiles ever will be saved";

—"Literally, Abraham was to be the father of many nations, but you make the Gentiles illegitimate, unplanned children";

—"You make types and shadows the body or substance itself, contrary to Colossians 2:17—it is contradictory to make the types and shadows a photograph, as if they were the very things they poorly picture."

Many more and better examples than the above paraphrases could be given, no doubt, yet "It is enough," as Jesus would say. But as for the photographic—Christ's wondrous developing, through the darkroom of the Cross, accomplished the transition of Covenants, transformed the typical into the higher application of that sense (Fairbairn), moved the focus from Old Testament shadows to the literal-yet-greater fulfillments: "the *mountain* of the Lord's house shall be established in the top of the *mountains* (Isaiah 2:2 KJV)"—Mount Zion becomes MOUNT ZION; Jerusalem below becomes JERUSALEM ABOVE; the Palestinian inheritance becomes "SHALL INHERIT THE EARTH"; the seed of Abraham as Jewish becomes CHRIST AND CHRISTIANS OF EVERY NATIONALITY; old Israel becomes NEW ISRAEL; sacrifices are ended by THE SACRIFICE; the temple of stones built upon rock is now the TEMPLE OF LIVING STONES BUILT UPON *THE* ROCK; the kingdom of David (Palestinian) became THE KINGDOM OF DAVID'S GREATER SON (UNIVERSAL).

To illustrate how something can be literal yet greater, consider: Brad wishes he had a car like Mike's, and lets it be known to dad. Dad says, "Well, Brad, graduation day is coming. I'll think about it." Dad thinks: A car like Mike's? why, it's a klunker! motor is done for, tires worn to the cords, upholstery shot, dents and dings, brakes down to the metal, a rattle trap. Graduation day arrives. Dad gives Brad the keys to a new car! Was this a literal fulfillment of Brad's hope? Yes, and then some!

Literalism without the interpretation of Christ and liberty of the Spirit, is blindness; this Old Testament veil is done away in Christ. In the New Covenant the people of God are ". . . the epistle of Christ . . . written not with ink, but with the Spirit of the living God; not in tables of stone, but in fleshy tables of the heart . . . not of the letter, but of the spirit: for the letter killeth, but the spirit giveth life" (2 Corinthians 3:3,6).

THE RESTITUTION OF ALL THINGS. Webster's Unabridged Dictionary beautifully defines *restitution* as "the final restoration of all things and persons to harmony with God's will." What is meant is the restoring of the eternal state as it was before the sin of fallen angels which was followed later by the sin of humankind. Restitution will fix eternal destinies, with creation itself delivered from the bondage of corruption (Romans 8:21). Restitution is the renovation of the whole creation. Matthew Henry rightly stated that it points to "the new heavens, and the new earth, which will be the product of the dissolution of all things." All evil will be put in its prepared place; all good will be put in its prepared place. Christ is the decisive factor involved. For some, only heaven will make amends; for others, only hell will repay. Restitution will be forever.

A predictable warp is found in the Scofield footnote to Acts 3:21 which it sees as meaning the restoration of Old Testament Israel. Its comment on the verse is: "The prophets speak of the restoration of Israel to the land . . . and of the restoration of the theocracy under David's son." Apart from the error, how shallow to think that a conversion of Jewish people living during an imagined 7-year future tribulation plus 1,000 years of heaven on earth (which, however, ends in rebellion) adds up to the restitution of all things!

These false teachings of a restoration of Old Testament Israel and a future Jewish conversion to Christ are the final wrong done to that distressed people. The restitution will be too late for all souls.

HARM AND HOPE AT HOME AND ABROAD. In the writer's hospital work, some needed counseling who had committed desperate acts, including the killing of loved ones, for fear of greater harm coming through 666, or police forces of antichrist, or other aberrations. Seeing such things in too fleshly a sense (as in 7-year tribulation teaching) takes it out of God's hands and puts it into ours, which proves too much for some to handle. The real truth of the historic faith is worse, namely that the End is at hand at all times, not scary myths; but this leaves it in God's hands, and is mentally as well as emotionally more healthy. Many patients, who all seemed to have seen the film "Thief in the Night," worriedly asked about the mark of the beast, the identity of antichrist, and similar concerns; some were startled at times, thinking they had missed the rapture.

Some years ago, a Christian worker from New Guinea wrote to the author: "This country is saturated with premillennial/dispensational views. I came here five years ago. It appears that, up until that time, every bookstore in the country pushed the books of Hal Lindsey and others; so I have a major task trying to re-direct people's thinking." The worker further explained: "Some months ago, I ordered forty copies of your book from Concordia and I expect them to arrive at any time. I obtained a smaller quantity by air mail and have given most of them away—mostly enclosing them with mail orders from customers who ask for the 'wrong' ones!"

On another front, a former Lutheran missionary to Argentina and Chile, wrote as follows: "After having waded through dozens of volumes on things to come for planet earth, your little book was like a breath of fresh air and it made more sense than anything else I had been able to come up with. Especially when one sees the teachings that are so rampant in many of the independent church groups functioning all about us nowadays, the position set forth in your book in such a clear and concise way is as I said, like a breath of fresh air."

The next paragraph is even more humbling and thrilling. "I took the liberty to translate seven chapters of your book into Spanish, and hereby send you the work I have done, in the hope that this beautiful little book might be published in Spanish some day." This retired missionary is still very active. He concluded by saying: "I leave this in your hands dear brother Plueger with the prayer that it might one day be accessible to thousands of searchers after the truth in Latin America and Spanish speaking countries of the world."

Since then, he has completed a Spanish translation of this revised edition, *Things to Come and Not to Come*. If you, dear reader, would pray for this Spanish edition to be published and made available, our Foundation would be most grateful. Our missionary brother expressed willingness to return on a teaching tour of South America with the message of this book. By faith we believe it is possible that Foundation materials can be ongoing and be available to other lands via workers. Editions and materials in other languages is a goal. Helpers welcome!

ALL IS NOT WELL IN ZION. In upholding the historic faith, the author means the Biblical, apostolic, creedal faith of roughly the first five Christian centuries, which faith today appears to be ignored by many inside and outside the Church. She must get back to upholding and proclaiming without compromise the inerrant Word and its cardinal doctrines. Pastors must insist on this, or lay people must insist on it if their pastors do not.

Till the kingdom comes in its heavenly form, every minister must heed St. Paul: "I charge you therefore before God, and the Lord Jesus Christ, who is about to judge living and dead according to his appearing and his kingdom, preach the word; be urgent in season, out of season; convict, rebuke, exhort, with all patience and teaching. For the time will come when they will not endure sound teaching; but accord-

99

ing to their own desires will heap up to themselves teachers, having the itching ear; and from the truth they will turn away the ear, and will be turned aside to myths" (2 Timothy 4:1–4).

In exposing modern myths, it is not the spirit of the writer to down literalism, only literalism unguided by our Lord Jesus Christ. With the historic faith and his ordination vows, the author adheres to the guiding rule: Literal wherever possible. Those who take the Bible literally are honored by this writer rather than those who turn the Word of the living God into one vast allegory without teeth. They will be judged with greater strictness than those who have been taught systems which are literalized into error.

The tragic truth is that the historic faith, by and large, is silent on eschatology today. Errorists have taken the field. They believe in the Lord's coming, believe in it fervently but incorrectly. Pastors of historic faith groups who have been sickened and turned off by such error are not thereby exempted from teaching last things rightly. If the shoe fits, reading minister, learn from a country preacher in Scotland who was given a much deserved vacation to Edinburgh by his appreciative congregation. Having his heart wholly in the Lord, he spent the vacation mostly visiting services in the grand city churches. Upon his return he was asked his impression as to those churches. He commented that they had splendid facilities and everything in good order. And as to the pastors? With some hesitancy he humbly observed that they were eloquent but that they seemed all to fly on one wing, "They preach our Lord's first coming but not his second." If these pages have awakened pastors to fly also on the other wing, as does the New Testament so prominently, this book's mission will have been multiplied.

The historic faith also must take the field from those enthusiasts who lose their bearings as to the Holy Spirit. Indeed, "Be filled with the Spirit" (Ephesians 5:18), but be sure it is the Spirit. Those ignorant of history are condemned to relive it; this is so also in church history. Pastors are urged to sell all you have and buy Eusebius (*Ecclesiastical History*, of the first three centuries) as a noted Lutheran preacher of Germany once said of Spurgeon. Therein you will read how even false Christian presbyters seduced people into their opinions, drawing away many of the church; of speaking and uttering strange things, and proclaiming what was contrary to the institutions that had prevailed in the church, as handed down and preserved in succession from the earliest times; of others again, elated as if by the Holy Spirit, and the prophetic gift, and not a little puffed up, forgetting the caution given by our Lord; of talkative teachers, pretending that they were sent from the

Lord; of delusions, trances, and the spirit of deception; of false predictions; of prophetesses who, as soon as they were filled with the spirit, abandoned their husbands; and so ad infinitum. Christian historians of that formative period demonstrated "the impropriety of a prophet's speaking in ecstasy, accompanied by want of all shame and fear." One stated, "They will never be able to show that any in the Old or New Testament were thus violently agitated and carried away in spirit."

Revival in the proper sense of the term, however, is the urgent need at all times in the historic church. "O LORD, revive Your work in the midst of the years!" (Habakkuk 3:2). Each must pray, "Revive it, beginning with me," until the historic truth produces in us as much fervency as in those who have been taught a mixture of truth and error, who are turned on by misleading events unneeded by true faith.

CONCLUSION—AN APPEAL. Things said in this book have deeply grieved many Scofield users; for that the author is sorry. The Scofield Bible is as precious as the Bible itself to millions. Were the differences not so serious, it would be best to keep still. Some say, Isn't the only important thing that we be ready for His Coming? The answer is, Yes and No. Dionysius, Bishop of Alexandria, facing schisms and apostasies of whole churches due to a deceased Bishop's book which taught an earthly millennium, reluctantly opposed this, but succeeded in overcoming it. Between A.D. 260-268, Dionysius penned two works titled, *On the Promises,* in which he stated, "But the truth is to be loved and honored before all." The mixture of truth and error today is similar but far more serious, and has spread through the four quarters of the globe. Never can it be overcome again except at the End; but a solemn duty is upon those of us who uphold "the faith which was once for all delivered to the saints" (Jude 3). Furthermore, what the historic faith taught originally is infinitely more crucial than the frightening fantasies of a nonexistent future tribulation, whether falsely thought of as before, during, or after a pre-End rapture.

Infinitely more crucial, because when Christ comes this life is over, this world is gone, the Bible declares. In that indescribable moment, all will know instantly that the things exposed in this book were deceptions. But it will be too late! If you believe, dear reader, with the historic faith that the physical End could come at THIS MOMENT, what happens then with the 7-year future tribulation idea, the future antichrist idea, the future Jewish evangelists idea, the future world conversion idea, the future millennium idea? They become meaningless at that moment!

Every sinner must pray always, "When He shall come with trumpet sound, Oh, may I then in Him be found, Clothed in His righteousness alone, Faultless to stand before the throne. On Christ, the solid Rock, I stand; All other ground is sinking sand." In these days of many false prophets and great deception, as Jesus foretold, every believer must heed His voice, "Behold, I come quickly; hold fast what you have, that no one take your crown" (Revelation 3:11).

How hold fast? It is said that certain chess players with great skill always play with their eyes closed and their faces turned toward the wall between moves. Such remember the entire board and all the pieces as they were after the last move; and upon returning to play see the effect of an opponent's move upon the whole chess-board. One such player said, "It is far easier to deceive me when I watch moves than otherwise." Lesson: Keep the *whole* in mind when dealing with a Bible passage or a claim. Inability or failure to do so, throughout church history has introduced error. Bear in mind that the devil deceives *by* the Bible; by twisting its interpretation. It has been said, error rides best on the back of truth.

Keep in mind the whole, with its absolutes (page 37). Look away from interpretations not found in the words of the Word Himself. He is Savior, but also the "Counselor"- Interpreter (Luke 24)-the very spirit *of* prophecy. Revelation 20 is from Him, 1:1! So its thousand years, for example, is unfathomable time (Psalm 90:4; 2 Peter 3:8), hinting a seeming delay of His soon return-in harmony with *all* His teachings.

Keep your eyes on Him, *not* on the Middle East, as some advise. Do not foolishly swallow conspiracy theories, which overlook God's control over the devil and all evil, lest you fail to see and praise the good and great things God is doing. Avoid any "Who teach thee more than He has taught, Tell more than He revealed, Preach tidings which He never brought, And read what He left sealed." As in a Latin saying: "He has learned much who is willing to be ignorant of those things which the great teacher does not choose to impart."

You of the Biblical, original, creedal faith, and every enlightened reader, rise up! An appeal in the Name of Him who is the truth: Please share the burden of the common faith at issue herein. Support the truth as much as error has been supported. Join the campaign for Truth versus mixtures of truth and error. Do help spread this book!

The final say is given to our great, ever-sooner coming Lord and Savior, Jesus Christ: "BE READY, FOR IN SUCH AN HOUR AS YOU THINK NOT, THE SON OF MAN IS COMING."

Bibliography

Allis, Oswald T. *Prophecy and the Church*. Nutley, New Jersey: Presbyterian and Reformed Publishing Co., 1945.

Barr, James. *Fundamentalism*. London: SCM Press Ltd., 1977.

Blackstone, W. E. *Jesus Is Coming*. Old Tappan, New Jersey: Fleming H. Revell Co., 1898.

Boettner, Loraine. *The Millennium*. Philadelphia: Presbyterian and Reformed Publishing Co., 1958.

Bright, John. *The Kingdom of God: The Biblical Concept and Its Meaning for the Church*. Nashville: Abingdon Press, 1953.

Cox, William E. *Biblical Studies in Final Things*. Nutley, New Jersey: Presbyterian and Reformed Publishing Co., 1964.

——————. *The Millennium*. Nutley, New Jersey: Presbyterian and Reformed Publishing Co., 1964.

Engelder, Theodore and Collaborators Arndt, Graebner, Mayer. *Popular Symbolics*. St. Louis: Concordia Publishing House, 1934.

Erdman, Charles R. *The Book of Ezekiel*. Princeton, New Jersey: Fleming H. Revell Company, 1956.

Eusebius. *Ecclesiastical History*. London: Samuel Bagster and Sons, 1847.

Feinberg, Charles L. *Premillennialism or Amillennialism*. Wheaton, Illinois: Van Kampen Press, 1954.

Grier, W. J. *Momentous Event*. London: The Banner of Truth Trust, 1945.

Hanson, Robert S. *The Future of the Great Planet Earth*. Minneapolis, Minnesota: Augsburg Publishing House, 1972.

Hendriksen, William. *More than Conquerors*. Grand Rapids, Michigan: Baker Book House, 1967, 1st ed. 1939.

Henry, Matthew. *Matthew Henry's Commentary,* Vol. VI. New York: Fleming H. Revell Company, [n.d.].

Holman, A. J. *Holman Study Bible—Revised Standard Version*. Philadelphia: A. J. Holman and Company, 1962.

Ironside, H. A. *Lectures on the Revelation*. New York: Loizeaux Brothers, 1920.

Ladd, George Eldon. *A Commentary on the Revelation of John*. Grand Rapids, Michigan: Wm. B. Eerdmans Publishing Co., 1972.

Lenski, R. C. H. *Interpretation of St. John's Revelation*. Columbus, Ohio: The Wartburg Press, 1943.

Lindsey, Hal and C. C. Carlson. *The Late Great Planet Earth*. Grand Rapids, Michigan: Zondervan Publishing House, 1970.

Little, C. H. *Explanation of the Book of Revelation*. St. Louis: Concordia Publishing House, 1950.

Lowry, Cecil John. *Christians Believe.* Oakland, California: Trinity Book Room, [n.d.].

_____. *Christian Catechism.* Oakland, California: Color Art Press, 1961.

Luther, Martin. *D. Martin Luthers Werke,* vol. 47. Weimar: Hermann Boehlaus Nachfolger, 1912.

MacPherson, Dave. *The Incredible Cover-Up.* Plainfield, New Jersey: Logos International, 1975.

Mauro, Philip. *The Gospel of the Kingdom.* Boston: Hamilton Brothers, 1928.

McClain, Alva J. *Daniel's Prophecy of the Seventy Weeks.* Grand Rapids, Michigan: Zondervan Publishing House, 1940.

Murray, George L. *Millennial Studies.* Grand Rapids, Michigan: Baker Book House, 1948.

Patton, William. *The Judgment of Jerusalem.* New York: Robert Carter and Brothers, 1877.

Pentecost, J. Dwight. *Things to Come.* Grand Rapids, Michigan: Zondervan Publishing House, 1958; rpt.

Pieper, Francis. *Christian Dogmatics.* St. Louis: Concordia Publishing House, 1950.

Ramm, Bernard. *Protestant Biblical Interpretation.* Grand Rapids, Michigan: Baker Book House, 1970.

Reu, M. *Lutheran Dogmatics.* Columbus, Ohio: Wartburg Press, 1951.

Sandeen, Ernest R. *The Roots of Fundamentalism.* Chicago: The University of Chicago Press, 1970.

Sauer, Erich. *The Triumph of the Crucified: A Survey of Historical Revelation in the New Testament,* trans. G. H. Lang, Grand Rapids, Michigan: Wm. B. Eerdmans Publishing Co., 1957.

Scofield, C. I., ed. *The Scofield Reference Bible.* New York: Oxford University Press, 1909.

The Septuagint Version of the Old Testament. New York: Harper & Brothers, [n.d.].

Spence, J. D. M., and Exell, Joseph S., eds. *The Pulpit Commentary,* Vol. XII. Grand Rapids, Michigan: William B. Eerdmans Publishing Co., 1950.

Spurgeon, Charles Haddon. *The Treasury of the Bible,* New Testament, Vol. IV. Grand Rapids, Michigan: Zondervan Publishing House, 1962.

Strong, Augustus Hopkins. *Outlines of Systematic Theology.* Philadelphia: American Baptist Publication Society, 1908.

Swete, Henry Barclay. *The Apocalypse of St. John.* Grand Rapids, Michigan: Wm. B. Eerdmans Publishing Co., 1951.

Thomas, Lawrence Rowe, *Does the Bible Teach Millennialism?* Swengel, Pa.: Reiner Publications [n.d.].

Young, Edward J. *The Prophecy of Daniel.* Grand Rapids, Michigan: William B. Eerdmans Publishing Co., 1949.

Notes

Introduction

1. All Bible quotations are from the *New American Standard Bible* or free unless otherwise indicated.
2. Pentecost, p. 372.
3. Boettner, p. 158.
4. Murray, p. 12.
5. Cox, *The Millennium*, p. 6.
6. Ibid., p. 15.
7. Ibid., p. 7.

Chapter 1

1. *Clavis Bibliorum* (1675). p. 10, cited by C. A. Briggs, *Biblical Study*, p. 363, quoted by Ramm, pp. 267-268.
2. Cox, *Biblical Studies in Final Things*, p. 39.
3. Feinberg, p. 126.
4. Cox, *The Millennium*, p. 57.
5. "A completely futuristic view of the kingdom (that in no sense does the kingdom now exist) and a completely spiritualized view of the kingdom (that the kingdom is solely the rule of God in the heart) are not true to the doctrinal teaching of the parables" (Ramm, p. 286).
6. Murray, p. 62. "The claim of modern dispensationalism is that Jesus Christ came to establish a Jewish kingdom upon the earth."
7. Allis, p. 83.
8. Scofield, p. 1027.
9. Allis, p. 75.
10. Grier, p. 61.
11. Scofield, p. 1026.
12. Ramm, p. 253.
13. Patton, pp. 59-60.
14. Eusebius, pp. 104-105.
15. Lowry, *Christian Catechism*, pp. 59-60.
16. Thomas, pp. 8-9.
17. Lowry, *Christian Catechism*, p. 62.
18. Allis, p. 312.
19. Thomas, pp. 3-4.
20. Murray, pp. 71-72.
21. Thomas, p. 8.
22. Ibid., p. 5.

Chapter 2

1. Bright, p. 86.
2. McClain, p. 13.
3. See Young, pp. 21–22.
4. Young, pp. 220–221.
5. Thomas, p. 97.
6. Thomas, p. 98.
7. A. J. Holman, *Holman Study Bible—Revised Standard Version* (Philadelphia: A. J. Holman and Company, 1962), p. 783b. Similar explanations are offered by others as follows: J. D. M. Spence and Joseph S. Exall, eds., *The Pulpit Commentary*, XII (Grand Rapids, Mich.: Wm. B. Eerdmans Publishing Company, 1950), p. xxxiii: "Whether . . . it ought to be concluded that the prophet anticipated a final ingathering of the Jews to Palestine, with Christ reigning as their Prince in Jerusalem, it would hardly be safe to affirm. . . ."; Charles R. Erdman, *The Book of Ezekiel* (Princeton, New Jersey: Fleming H. Revell Company, 1956), p. 124: "These future glories chapter 40–48 were sketched by the prophet in figures."
8. Grier, p. 56.

Chapter 3

1. Pentecost, p. 110.
2. Grier, p. 46.
3. Thomas, p. 9.
4. Grier, p. 74.
5. Hendriksen, p. 7.
6. Ladd, p. 261.
7. Swete, p. xliii.
8. Eusebius, p. 307.
9. Thomas, p. 16.

Chapter 4

1. Cox, *The Millennium*, p. 40.
2. Eusebius, pp. 120–121.
3. Thomas, p. 25.
4. Ibid., p. 92.
5. Grier, p. 24.
6. Eusebius, pp. 143–144.
7. Grier, p. 25.
8. Ibid.
9. Ibid., p. 27.
10. Eusebius, p. 305.
11. Grier, p. 27.
12. Ibid., p. 28.
13. Ibid., p. 29.

14. Ibid.
15. Weimar ed., vol. 47, p. 561.
16. Grier, p. 30.
17. Murray, p. 15.

Chapter 5

1. Henry, p. 1179.
2. Ramm, p. xv.
3. *The Ante-Nicene Fathers*, VII, 358.
4. Scofield, p. 1228.
5. Ladd, p. 271.

Chapter 6

1. Scofield, p. 1343.
2. Sauer, p. 152.
3. Allis, p. 2.
4. Lowry, *Christian Believe*, pp. 20–22.
5. Lowry, *Christian Catechism*, p. 64.

Chapter 7

1. Grier, p. 62.
2. Feinberg, pp. 174–175.
3. Thomas, p. 79.
4. Ironside, pp. 128–129.

Chapter 8

1. Grier, p. 15.
2. Strong, p. 264.
3. Strong, p. 263.

Chapter 9

1. Murray, p. 131.
2. Grier, p. 66.
3. Spurgeon, p. 463.
4. Ibid., p. 464.

Chapter 11

1. Murray, p. 23.
2. Hendriksen, p. 234.

Chapter 13

1. Grier, p. 121.
2. Grier, pp. 123–124.

1. Murray, p. 123.

Index of Main Bible Passages

Index of Subjects

STATEMENT OF TRUTHS

With the historic church, we believe from all the Bible that:

1. our Lord Jesus Christ is coming, not secretly but visibly and once only, at a time no one knows;
2. the world ends as Christ comes, with the saved caught away (raptured) as the universe is destroyed and refashioned;
3. in that same moment, all humanity of history will be raised to stand before God at one judgment;
4. the door of salvation will be closed forever at Christ's coming;
5. all not won before that moment are lost forever;
6. the millennium, according to all Scripture and the structure of the Book of Revelation, is not future but signifies the gospel reign of Christ, during which the deceiver, Satan, has been restrained;
7. heaven is assured all in Christ Jesus, God the Son, while hell awaits all not converted to Him in the present time of grace.

"For God so loved the world, that he gave his only begotten Son, that whoever believes in him should not perish, but have everlasting life."— John 3:16

The Statement of Truths was drafted at Oakland, California, 1973, in a series of luncheon meetings by concerned ministers, including the Dean of a Greek Orthodox cathedral, a Roman Catholic Monsignor, several Lutheran, Anglican, Methodist, Presbyterian, Reformed, a professor from a Bay Area Baptist seminary, and a former dispensationalist Assembly of God principal who served as Chairman, with the author of this book serving as Secretary. The Statement was to serve as a guide for public conferences on Things to Come.

TRUTH versus Truth and Error

A Foundation for the Historic Faith on Last Things